D1071833

BIBLIOGRAPHICAL SERIES

from the Yale University Library Collections

A BIBLIOGRAPHY OF

James Joyce

[1882–1941]

JOHN J. SLOCUM

AND HERBERT CAHOON

NEW HAVEN:

YALE UNIVERSITY PRESS, 1953

Printed in the United States of America by the Vail-Ballou Press, Inc., Binghamton, N. Y.

Library of Congress Catalog Card Number: 52-13968

PREFACE

THIS BIBLIOGRAPHY is based on the Joyce Library formed during the past fifteen years by John J. Slocum, Tuxedo Park, New York, which is now in the Yale University Library. The compilation of the bibliography has taken nearly ten years of investigation, research, and preparation of copy, but there are, nevertheless, many points at which we feel it to be incomplete. The present book covers the publication of works by Joyce to the year 1950, with occasional subsequent additions as they have come to our attention. Some of the sections, particularly the translations into foreign languages, are not fully developed, and we look forward to the opportunity of completing them at some future time. We regret that we could not include the many thousands of books, periodicals, and newspapers which we have gathered concerning Joyce biography and criticism, but we hope to publish these, as well as a detailed chronology of Joyce's life, at a later date.

Full bibliographical descriptions have been made of all first editions and other items of importance. The compilers have considered an edition to be all copies printed from one setting of type. Sizes have been given in centimeters, i.e., sizes of the leaves and not of the bindings; the back covers of the bindings are blank unless otherwise stated. Except for title pages and bindings, data from the books described, such as copyright statements, colophons, and limitation notices, are given uniformly in italics. Papers are without watermarks unless so indicated in the collation. Whenever possible, authorities for information have been given; dates of publication have been taken from the records of the individual publishers or from the published records of the U.S. Copyright Office. In spite of our considerable efforts, we have found that some information was not available, and we will welcome any assistance, suggestions, or corrections which may be offered.

Among the books referred to in the collations and text are:

Gheerbrant, Bernard, compiler. *James Joyce: Sa Vie, Son Œuvre, Son Rayonnement.* Paris, La Hune, 1949. This work is also referred to as the La Hune Catalogue; the collection now in the

Lockwood Memorial Library, University of Buffalo, Buffalo, New York, is referred to as the Joyce Paris Library.

Gorman, Herbert. *James Joyce.* New York, Farrar & Rinehart, [1939]. This work is referred to as Gorman, 1939.

Joyce, Stanislaus. *Recollections of James Joyce by His Brother.* New York, The James Joyce Society, 1950.

The abbreviation FW has been used for *Finnegans Wake*, RH for the Random House and Modern Library editions of *Ulysses*, and H for the B. W. Huebsch edition of *A Portrait of the Artist as a Young Man*, New York, 1916.

There have been many moments of exasperation and discouragement during the compilation of this bibliography; these would have been difficult to overcome had it not been for the constant and continued help of many friends and associates whose interest in and knowledge of James Joyce and his work have been truly invaluable to us. We wish to thank them for their assistance, to acknowledge that they are responsible for much of whatever merit this book may contain, and to state that for any errors or omissions we alone are responsible.

We have consulted the following bibliographies of Joyce and make acknowledgment to them here:

O'Hegarty, P. S. *A Bibliography of James Joyce.* Dublin, A. Thom, [1946]. Reprinted from *Dublin Magazine*, Dublin, N.S. XXI.1 (Jan.–Mar. 1946) 38–47.

Parker, Alan. *James Joyce: A Bibliography of His Writings, Critical Material and Miscellanea.* Boston, F. W. Faxon, 1948.

Roberts, R. F. "Bibliographical Notes on James Joyce's 'Ulysses.'" *Colophon*, New York, N.S. I.4 (Spring, 1936) 565–79.

Spoerri, James Fuller. *Catalog of a Collection of the Works of James Joyce Exhibited at the Newberry Library.* Chicago, privately printed by the author, 1948.

White, William. "James Joyce: Addenda to Alan Parker's Bibliography." *Bibliographical Society of America.* Papers, New York, XLIII (fourth quarter 1949) 401–11.

Students may be interested to know that the works by Parker, Spoerri, and White contain listings of critical material.

In the early stages of compilation of this bibliography the late

Alida S. Livingston gathered and arranged much information that became the foundation from which the work proceeded. Her great interest, knowledge, and enthusiasm have been sorely missed. Dr. R. F. Roberts, formerly of the Collectors' Bookshop and Seven Gables Bookshop, gave generously of his time and extensive knowledge of modern literature to this book. His "Bibliographical Notes on James Joyce's 'Ulysses,'" listed above, was largely responsible for the inception of this bibliography in the spring of 1938. Much of his work is still incorporated here and we wish to record our deep regret that he was unable to continue as coauthor.

Harriet Shaw Weaver, Oxford, England, with characteristic generosity and modesty, has made available to us, through records she has preserved and through her own valuable recollections, a treasure house of information. Her incredible foresight and firm belief in Joyce as a writer led her to subscribe to two clipping services for material concerning him from about 1916 to 1948 and she has thus preserved ephemera which might otherwise have been lost forever. These clippings are now in the Yale University Library.

Stanislaus Joyce, Trieste, brother of James Joyce, has furnished the authors with otherwise unprocurable information about Joyce's early newspaper contributions, ephemera, manuscripts, and life in Trieste.

Sylvia Beach, Paris, Joyce's friend and publisher of *Ulysses*, has contributed many items and much information without which Joyce's bibliography would be woefully incomplete.

James F. Spoerri, Chicago, whose unfailing kindness and enthusiasm have been a constant inspiration, must be given special mention for the vast amount of essential bibliographical notation he has contributed from his own fine Joyce collection and his vast knowledge of the subject.

Quentin Keynes, New York, has shared many fine Joyce items and bibliographical points which do credit to his perception and intuition as a collector.

We have used the facilities of the New York Public Library almost daily in the preparation of this bibliography. Virtually every department of this institution, particularly the Information Division, Main Reading Room, and Photographic Service and Work Shop, has given us generous assistance and valuable advice. The Library of Congress, the libraries of Yale, Harvard, and Princeton Universities and the University of Buffalo, the Cleveland Public Library, the Boston Public Library, and the Pierpont Morgan Library, New York, have given help at many crucial stages. We have also used the British Museum, the Bodleian Library, the National Library of Ireland, the Bibliothèque Nationale, Paris, the Biblioteca Civica, Trieste, and the Vatican Library.

Our many benefactors in the United States and Canada include Ellsworth Mason, Joseph Prescott, Frances Steloff, John H. Thompson, Richard M. Kain, Donald C. Gallup, Norman Holmes Pearson, T. E. Hanley, Ben Abramson, Samuel Roth, Mr. and Mrs. Padraic Colum, William Y. Tindall, James T. Babb, Lewis M. Stark, B. W. Huebsch, Herbert Gorman, David Randall, Charles D. Abbott, John S. Van E. Kohn, Michael Papantonio, James Laughlin, A. M. Klein, Frederick R. Goff, Mrs. Vincent R. Impellitteri, Wirth Howell, Alexander Buchman, William A. Jackson, H. K. Croessmann, Renato Poggioli, P. J. Conkwright, Anna Heifetz, Random House, the Viking Press, Princeton University Press, Yale University Press, Mrs. Frank McMullan, Avrahm Yarmolinsky, and Marjorie Wynne.

In Europe we are indebted to Stuart Gilbert, Lucie Noel (Mme Paul L. Léon), Frank Budgen, Alfred L. Grigis, Maria Jolas, Seumas O'Sullivan, Richard J. Hayes, Bertram Rota, Claud Sykes, Henry Gerson, Niall Sheridan, Constantine P. Curran, the late Carlo Linati, Owen Sheehy Skeffington, P. S. O'Hegarty, George D. Painter, Liam O'Briain, Patricia Hutchins, Faber & Faber, Lionel Monro, and Percy Muir.

Sho Kajima of Tokyo, Japan, has kindly provided us with copies of many of Joyce's publications in Japanese and information concerning them.

J. J. S.
H. C.

Bonn, Germany
and
New York, New York
November 15, 1952

CONTENTS

A. *Books and Pamphlets by James Joyce*

1. [ET TU, HEALY!] [1891 *or* 1892]

No copy of this broadside or pamphlet is known to exist. Joyce stated that he wrote it at the age of nine and that his father had copies printed and distributed among his friends. The subject of this work was Timothy Michael Healy (1855–1931), later governor general of the Irish Free State, who turned against Charles Stewart Parnell (1846–91) at the time of his downfall. Gorman gives the printer of *Et Tu, Healy!* as Alleyn and O'Reilly. This firm (actually Alley and O'Reilly) was traced through a series of mergers to the Temple Press; a director of this press stated that all records of the earlier printers were destroyed during Easter Week in 1916.

That this broadside or pamphlet really existed is further substantiated by a letter from Joyce to Miss Harriet Weaver, November 22, 1930, in which he states that he has incorporated his verse written at the age of nine in Chapter I, Part II, of *Finnegans Wake* (FW 231). The original lines as Joyce wrote them to Miss Weaver are:

> My cot alas that dear old shady home
> Where oft in youthful sport I played
> Upon thy verdant grassy fields all day
> Or lingered for a moment in thy bosom shade.

Stanislaus Joyce has graciously permitted quotation concerning this work from the unpublished manuscript of his forthcoming book. He also recalls the line "My cot, alas! the dear old shady home" and goes on to say:

At the end of the piece the dead Chief is likened to an eagle, looking down on the grovelling mass of Irish politicians from [as he recalls]:

> "His quaint-perched aerie on the crags of Time
> Where the rude din of this . . . century
> Can trouble him no more."

My father had it printed and distributed the broadsheets to admirers. I have a distinct recollection of my father's bringing home a roll of thirty or forty of them. Parnell, however, died when we were still at Bray, so the piece must have been written some months or a year after Parnell's death, because I am positive that the broadsheet was printed when we were living at Blackrock. My brother was, therefore, between nine and ten years of age when his ambition to be a writer bore its first timid blossom.

Concerning the title (the work is also known as the Parnell Pamphlet) Stanislaus Joyce writes: "I see mentioned, apparently with my brother's sanction, the title of 'Et Tu, Healy,' though I do not remember that it bore that title."

Further references to this work may be found in Gorman (B 6), p. 235; Gorman, 1939, p. 36; James Joyce, *Dubliners*, New York, Modern Library, 1926, pp. ix–x (introduction by Padraic Colum); Stanislaus Joyce, *Recollections of James Joyce*, p. 6, and in unpublished letters from Constantine P. Curran and P. S. O'Hegarty in the Slocum Library.

2. THE HOLY OFFICE [1904 *or* 1905]

First edition:

THE HOLY OFFICE. | [*decorative rule*]

COLLATION: A broadside, 28.9 x 22.1 cm. Printed on white wove paper watermarked: [spread eagle] | L. P. [in script] | Mercantil Eagle Paper

PAGINATION: Caption title as above, followed by a poem of 96 lines printed in two columns and separated by a vertical rule. Printed signature at bottom of second column: *James A. Joyce.*

PUBLICATION DATE AND PRICE: Printed in Pola (then part of the Austro-Hungarian Empire) late in 1904 or early in 1905. Joyce was in Pola from November 1904 to March 1905 and had copies printed during this period. He presumably mailed copies to a number of people in Ireland and also had copies distributed there; the Keller copy described by P. S. O'Hegarty in his *Bibliography of James Joyce* bears the manuscript date 1905. The broadside was printed at Joyce's expense and distributed free.

NUMBER OF COPIES: Not ascertained, but probably less than 100.

NOTES: A letter from George Hetherington, Dublin, December 3, 1949, gives the following information about the copy of *The Holy Office* described by O'Hegarty:

> I am afraid I have no real evidence to submit regarding the printing of *The Holy Office;* but there is a very strong supposition that it was printed in Dublin before he left. I know that my father-in-law (T. G. Keller) used to relate that Joyce himself distributed the leaflets into the letter-boxes of his friends just before he left.

The type font and the semi-inverted quotation marks used in this broadside, however, are characteristic of Continental printing.

Stanislaus Joyce has written the compilers that *The Holy Office* was printed twice, once in Dublin and once in Pola. He writes: "The Dublin publisher, not being paid, refused to deliver the goods and owing to his insolent letter, my brother, when he had the money, preferred to have it printed again in Pola. The printer's letter requested him to remove his 'literature'." A letter from the Dublin Printing and Litho. Co. to James Joyce, 60 Shelburne Road, Dublin, August 17, 1904, asking him to correct the proof of *The Holy Office* and return it is in the Slocum Library.

In another letter Stanislaus Joyce writes: "The distribution of the copies printed I think in Pola, was done, of course, by me. I recollect delivering it first to the man mentioned, Keller—a very decent fellow—at Hely's, the Stationers, in Dame Street, where he was manager."

Since no copies of the Dublin printing of *The Holy Office* seem to have survived, the Pola printing may be considered to be the first edition.

The Holy Office is included in *The Portable James Joyce* (A 55), *The Essential James Joyce* (A 56), and Gorman, 1939, pp. 138–41.

3. CHAMBER MUSIC 1907

First edition:

1907 | CHAMBER | MUSIC | BY | JAMES JOYCE | ELKIN MATHEWS | VIGO STREET, LONDON

[Note: The foregoing is within an elaborate design which includes columns, a harpsichord, and drapery and scrolls with simulated musical notations.]

COLLATION: [40] pp. [A]^4, B–E^4. 16.2 x 11 cm., top and bottom edges trimmed, fore edge untrimmed. Printed on white laid paper.

PAGINATION: p.[1], fly title; p.[2], blank; p.[3], title page; p.[4], printer: *Gilbert & Rivington Ltd. Clerkenwell, London, E.C.* ; pp. [5–40], text, poems numbered consecutively from I to XXXVI.

BINDING: Light green cloth, gilt stamped. Front cover: CHAMBER | MUSIC | JAMES JOYCE Spine, reading from bottom to top: CHAMBER MUSIC JAMES JOYCE [publisher's imprint stamped horizontally at foot:] ELKIN | MATHEWS Issued in transparent tissue protective wrapper.

PUBLICATION DATE AND PRICE: May 1907. 1*s*. 6*d*. The London 1918 edition of *Chamber Music* (A 4) lists May 1907 as the publication date of the first edition. The British Museum copy (destroyed during World War II) was received May 8, 1907; the copy at the Bodleian Library, Oxford, was received May 11, 1907. The earliest publication notice located is in the *Athenaeum*, London, 4150 (May 11, 1907) 577. Gorman, 1939, p. 191, lists April 6, 1907, as the publication date. This date was given to him by Arthur Symons; Symons unquestionably received an advance review copy of *Chamber Music*. His review appeared in the *Nation*, London, 1.17 (June 22, 1907) 639.

NUMBER OF COPIES: 509, according to Gorman, 1939, p. 191.

NOTES: Three binding variants, distinguished most easily by the type of end papers used, have been noted:

First variant: Thick laid end papers with horizontal chain lines. 16.2 x 11 cm. Poems in signature C well centered on page.

Second variant: Thick wove end papers. 15.8 x 11 cm. Poems in signature C poorly centered on page.

Third variant: Thin wove transparent end papers. 15.9 x 10.9 cm. Poems in signature C poorly centered on page.

The priority of the second and third variants is undetermined. The binding of the first variant is of a slightly lighter shade of green than that of the later variants. The points of the first variant are to be found in the Forrest Reid copy dated June 15, 1907, and the personal copy of Elkin Mathews, both in the Slocum Library; in the presentation copy to Arthur Symons, inscribed "To Arthur Symons 14.V.07. Jas. A. Joyce," which was sold at the Parke-Bernet Galleries, New York, December 3, 1951, item No. 561 in the Litchfield Sale; and in the copy in the Bodleian Library, Oxford. Only one copy of the second variant has been examined; its provenance is unknown. The points of the third variant are to be found in presentation copies signed by Joyce on May 25, 1928, and in 1929. These copies are in the Slocum Library.

Arthur Symons, to whom Yeats introduced Joyce in December 1902, was responsible for the publication of *Chamber Music* and for much of the praise it received. Symons submitted the manuscript to Grant Richards for Joyce in September 1904. When Richards re-

CHAMBER MUSIC. 1907. A3.

fused to publish it without a subsidy from Joyce, Symons offered it to Constable. Eventually Elkin Mathews accepted and published it at Symons' urging. Symons also gave it the very favorable review cited above.

Joyce never received royalties for *Chamber Music*, although he claimed in a letter to Elkin Mathews that his contract called for payments after the sale of 300 copies. In 1912 Joyce himself undertook the sale of copies in Trieste with considerable success.

The original contract for the publication of *Chamber Music*, dated January 17, 1907, is in the Yale University Library.

For poems from *Chamber Music* first published in periodicals see C 26, 27, 28, and 31. See also B 2.

4. CHAMBER MUSIC 1918

Second edition (London):

CHAMBER | MUSIC | BY | JAMES JOYCE | LONDON | ELKIN MATHEWS, CORK STREET | M CM XVIII

COLLATION: [40] pp. $[A]^8$, C^8, D^4 (B not used). 17.3 x 11.9 cm., top edge trimmed, other edges untrimmed. Printed on white laid paper, watermarked: [crown] | *Abbey Mills* | *Greenfield*

PAGINATION: p.[1], fly title; p.[2], statement of edition: *First Published . . . May 1907* | *Second Edition . . . January 1918* ; p.[3], title page; p.[4], blank; pp.[5–39], text, poems numbered consecutively from I to XXXVI; p.[40], advertisement and printer: *Chamber Music . . . Some Press Notices* [24 lines], at bottom: *London, Printed by William Clowes and Sons, Limited* .

BINDING: Gray laid paper covers, printed in black. Front cover: CHAMBER | MUSIC | JAMES JOYCE Spine, reading from bottom to top: CHAMBER MUSIC JAMES JOYCE [publisher's imprint stamped horizontally at foot] ELKIN | MATHEWS

PUBLICATION DATE AND PRICE: January 1918. 1*s.* 3*d.* paper; 2*s.* cloth.

NUMBER OF COPIES: Not ascertained.

NOTES: Not seen in cloth binding; possibly copies of the 1907 edition were used to supply this demand.

Poems XXI and XXII were combined on the same page to leave p. [40] free for the advertisement.

A third English edition of 500 copies of *Chamber Music* was issued by the Egoist Press, London, in August 1923. *Chamber Music* was acquired from the Egoist Press by Jonathan Cape, Ltd., in 1924; 393 sets of sheets were turned over to them at that time. The first Cape edition was issued in 1927; reprinted in 1934, 1943, 1945 (or 1946), 1949, and 1950.

Chamber Music is included in *The Essential James Joyce* (A 56).

5. CHAMBER MUSIC [1918]

First American edition (Boston):

CHAMBER MUSIC | BY | JAMES JOYCE | [publisher's emblem] | THE CORNHILL COMPANY | BOSTON

COLLATION: [40] pp. [1–2]^8, [3]^4. 15.5 x 10.8 cm., top edge trimmed, other edges untrimmed. Printed on white laid paper.

PAGINATION: p.[1], fly title; p.[2], blank; p.[3], title page; p.[4], blank; pp.[5–40], text, poems numbered consecutively from I to XXXVI.

BINDING: Green cloth, gilt stamped. Front cover: CHAMBER | MUSIC | JAMES JOYCE Issued in transparent tissue protective wrapper.

PUBLICATION DATE AND PRICE: 1918. $1. Earliest review noted: *New York Call (The Call Magazine)*, June 22, 1918, p. 15.

NUMBER OF COPIES: Not ascertained, probably about 1,000.

NOTES: This unauthorized first American edition of *Chamber Music* was printed for Alfred Bartlett of the Cornhill Company. The compilers of this bibliography have been unable to obtain any information about Bartlett or details of publication of this book.

Copies with wove and with laid end papers have been noted; priority undetermined. There are also variations in the sharpness of the gilt stamping.

6. CHAMBER MUSIC 1918

First authorized American edition (New York):

CHAMBER MUSIC | BY JAMES JOYCE | AUTHORIZED EDITION PUBLISHED BY | B. W. HUEBSCH NEW YORK MCMXVIII | [publisher's emblem]
[Note: The foregoing is within a single-rule box.]

COLLATION: [48] pp. [1–3]^8. 17.5 x 12.1 cm., top edge gilt, other edges untrimmed. Printed on cream-white wove paper watermarked:

D [within diamond] | *Regal Antique* Cream-white end papers.

PAGINATION: pp.[1–2], blank; p.[3], fly title; p.[4], list of *Books by James Joyce* ; p.[5], title page; p.[6], copyright notice: *Copyright, 1918, by B. W. Huebsch* | *Printed in U.S.A.* ; p.[7], *Publisher's Note* | *This is the only American edition of* | *Chamber Music that is authorized by Mr.* | *Joyce.* ; p.[8], blank; p.[9], half-title; p.[10], blank; pp.[11–46], text, poems numbered consecutively from I to XXXVI; pp.[47–8], blank.

BINDING: Dark brown boards. Front cover, gilt stamped: CHAMBER MUSIC *by* JAMES JOYCE Spine, stamped in blind, reading from top to bottom: CHAMBER MUSIC *by* JAMES JOYCE

PUBLICATION DATE AND PRICE: September 30, 1918. $1.

NUMBER OF COPIES: Not ascertained.

NOTES: This authorized edition of *Chamber Music* was reprinted by B. W. Huebsch, Inc., in 1923 bound in black boards, the text being reset. Reset and reprinted by the Viking Press, New York, in August 1932, carrying the erroneous statement that it is the second American edition. The similarity of the roman numerals MCMXVIII and MCMXXIII in the same position on the title pages of the first two editions caused the true second authorized American edition to be overlooked.

Chamber Music is included in *Collected Poems* (A 44, 45) and in *The Portable James Joyce* (A 55).

7. GAS FROM A BURNER 1912

First edition:

GAS FROM A BURNER.

COLLATION: A broadside, 58.8 x 23 cm., printed on white wove paper.

PAGINATION: Caption title as above, followed by a poem of 98 lines. At bottom: James Joyce. | *Flushing, September 1912.*

PUBLICATION DATE AND PRICE: Published after September 1912. Distributed free.

NUMBER OF COPIES: Not ascertained. There were approximately ten copies in the Joyce Paris Library.

NOTES: On the Esher-Randle-Keynes-Spoerri copy of this broadside is the following holograph note in ink by Joyce:

This pasquinade was written in the railway station waiting room at Flushing, Holland on the way to Trieste from Dublin after the malicious burning of the 1st edition of *Dubliners* (1000 copies less one in my possession) by the printer Messrs John Falconer. Upper Sackville Street Dublin in July 1912.

The fact that Flushing appears on the broadside has resulted in Flushing's being given as the place of printing. Stanislaus Joyce says that it was printed in Trieste.

Gas from a Burner is included in *The Portable James Joyce* (A 55) and *The Essential James Joyce* (A 56).

8. DUBLINERS 1914

First edition:

DUBLINERS | BY | JAMES JOYCE | [ornamental leaf] | LONDON | GRANT RICHARDS LTD. | PUBLISHERS

COLLATION: 280 pp. $[A]^8$, $B–R^8$, S^4. 19 x 12.5 cm., all edges trimmed. Printed on cream-white laid paper; cream-white wove end papers.

PAGINATION: pp.[1–2], blank; p.[3], fly title; p.[4], publisher's advertisements [18 lines]; p.[5], title page; p.[6], printer: *Printed by the Riverside Press Limited | Edinburgh, Scotland | 1914* ; p. 7, *Contents* ; p.[8], blank; pp. 9–278, text; pp.[279–80], blank.

BINDING: Dark red cloth, gilt stamped. Front cover: DUBLINERS Spine: DUBLINERS | JAMES | JOYCE | GRANT RICHARDS Issued in green dust wrapper, printed in black.

PUBLICATION DATE AND PRICE: June 15, 1914. 3*s.* 6*d.*

NUMBER OF COPIES: 1,250 sets of sheets were printed, of which approximately 746 were bound in this edition.

NOTES: This first edition of *Dubliners* was preceded by two abortive printings which were not published. These were printed by Grant Richards in 1906 and by Maunsel, Dublin, in 1910.

Dubliners was offered to Grant Richards on October 15, 1905. At that time Joyce described it as a collection of twelve stories ("Two Gallants," "A Little Cloud," and "The Dead" were not completed) and went on to write:

I do not think that any writer has yet presented Dublin to the world. It has been a capital of Europe for thousands of years, it is supposed to be the second city of the British Empire and it is nearly three times as big as Venice. Moreover, on account of many circumstances which I cannot detail here the expression "Dubliner" seems to me to have some meaning and I doubt whether the same can be said for such words as "Londoner" and "Parisian" both of which have been used by writers as titles. From time to time I see in publishers' lists announcements of books on Irish subjects so that I think people might be willing to pay for the special odour of corruption which, I hope, floats over my stories.

Joyce mailed *Dubliners* to Richards on November 28, 1905, and in February 1906 it was accepted. On February 22 Joyce mailed "Two Gallants." By April Joyce's troubles with Richards and the English printers had begun. An extended account of this episode appears in Gorman, 1939, pp. 145–58, 169–74.

Meanwhile Richards had announced *Dubliners* for publication in his *First Catalogue of Books Published by Grant Richards . . .* [March] 1906, with an entry: "Joyce, James A. Dubliners. Crown 8vo. cloth. 5s."

The only surviving fragment of this edition is in the Houghton Library, Harvard University. It consists of two pages of page proof from "Two Gallants" and a manuscript reader's report of one and one-half pages recommending that the book be published. The proof pages are numbered 12 and 13; in the published (1914) version of "Two Gallants" the text of these two pages is considerably expanded. A pencil note on the margin of the proof reads: "We cannot print this. J A [?] April 17, 1906."

On May 5 Joyce, in a letter to Richards, defended his writing of *Dubliners* against the printers' objections:

> My intention was to write a chapter of the moral history of my country and I chose Dublin for the scene because that city seemed to me the centre of paralysis. I have tried to present it to the indifferent public under four of its aspects: childhood, adolescence, maturity and public life. The stories are arranged in this order. I have written it for the most part in a style of scrupulous meanness . . .

Joyce followed this up several letters later with another statement about the book as a whole: "It is not my fault that the odour of ashpits and old weeds and offal hangs round my stories. I seriously believe that you will retard the course of civilisation in Ireland by preventing the Irish people from having one good look at themselves in my nicely polished looking-glass."

Although Joyce made many concessions, Richards was not satisfied and this edition was abandoned before the end of 1906.

Apparently Joyce offered *Dubliners* to Elkin Mathews in 1907 after the publication of *Chamber Music*, for it was rejected sometime before February 1908. During this month Joyce wrote to ask that the manuscript be returned to him and not sent directly to Maunsel.

Gorman, 1939, p. 174, gives an amusing account of Joyce's negotiations with the English publisher John Long, who also rejected *Dubliners*.

There is no record of Joyce's negotiations with Maunsel concerning *Dubliners* until September 3, 1909, at which time he wrote to Molyneux Palmer of its acceptance. On April 4, 1910, he wrote Elkin Mathews that *Dubliners* was scheduled for publication in June. In June Joyce still expected immediate publication. He wrote to Molyneux Palmer that he was busy correcting proof and to Adolph Mann on June 24 that the book would be out in July. The firm of Maunsel in their 1910 catalogue, *Books by Irish Writers and Books about Ireland*, announced it as follows: "Dubliners. A book of short stories. By James Joyce. Author of 'Chamber Music.' 3s 6d. net." An account of the history of this printing in Joyce's own words appears in the *Egoist*, London, I.2 (Jan 15, 1914) 26–7, under the title "A Curious History" and is reprinted in Gorman, 1939, pp. 206–8.

The book was printed in an edition of 1,000 copies in July 1910 by John Falconer (present address, 2 Crow St., Dublin). The entire edition with the exception of the page proofs mentioned below was later burned by the printer because of "objectionable" passages in some of the stories. A complete set of page proofs was retained by Joyce, who, in the late 20's or early 30's turned them over to Sylvia Beach for sale. The set was sent to the United States to find a purchaser, but there is no record of a sale and the proofs may have been returned to Joyce. At least two other partial sets of proofs are in existence. In the Slocum Library are galley sheets of "A Mother," dated June 8, 1910, and "The Dead" (the last two pages missing), dated June 17, 1910, and page proofs of "Ivy Day in the Committee Room." An incomplete set of page proofs is also in the library of a London collector. This set includes "The Sisters," "An Encounter," "Eveline," "After the Race," "The Boarding House," "A Little Cloud," "Counterparts," "Clay," "A Painful Case," and a portion of "The Dead." The firm of John Falconer in Dublin advised the compilers that records no longer exist concerning the printing and subsequent burning of *Dubliners*.

While in negotiation with Maunsel, Joyce had circulated the letter (later to be known as *A Curious History*) about his publishing troubles. It is dated August 18, 1911. Even this letter had no effect and it was suggested that Dublin Castle, as a gesture of appeasement to an organization of Catholic laity with censorial interests, had ordered the suppression. September 1912 marked the end of negotiations.

In 1913 Elkin Mathews again turned down *Dubliners;* this only increased the firmness of Joyce's stand that his manuscript should undergo no changes. On November 23, 1913, he once again offered it to Grant Richards, guaranteed the sale of 120 copies in Trieste, and offered the set of Maunsel proofs to be used in setting up the edition. By the end of January 1914 Richards had accepted the book, and shortly afterward Joyce forwarded the proofs. On March 4, 1914, Joyce signed the contract and returned it to Richards. This contract, now in the Slocum Library, stipulates that no royalties will be paid on the first 500 copies and states that Joyce guarantees to purchase 120 copies. There is no mention of an advance, and Richards had the refusal of all Joyce's works for the next five years.

Joyce's troubles did not end with the publication of *Dubliners* on June 15, 1914. Richards was extremely remiss in paying him royalties and could not be persuaded to publish a second edition even after the sale of 504 sets of sheets to B. W. Huebsch, New York, in the autumn of 1916 had used up most of his copies while the demand for them continued. Finally, in order to hold Joyce, Richards reluctantly agreed to issue a second edition of *Dubliners* in 1918. This he did by importing sheets of the 1917 American edition from B. W. Huebsch and binding up just enough sets to satisfy Joyce. It is not known how many copies of this second Grant Richards edition of *Dubliners* exist, but it is scarce and only two copies have been reported in the last twelve years. One of these, the Edward W. Titus copy, is now in the Slocum Library.

It has been reported that in 1915 Grant Richards sold without Joyce's knowledge 500 sets of *Dubliners* sheets to Albert and Charles Boni of New York who had recently published *Des Imagistes* (B 4). A new title page was prepared with the New York imprint, and 499 copies were shipped to New York on the S.S. *Arabic* which was torpedoed in August 1915. All copies were lost except one which Albert Boni kept in his personal possession. He was unable to locate this copy in time for the compilers of this bibliography to examine it.

CONTENTS: Fifteen short stories: "The Sisters"; "An Encounter"; "Araby"; "Eveline"; "After the Race"; "Two Gallants"; "The Boarding House"; "A Little Cloud"; "Counterparts"; "Clay"; "A Painful Case"; "Ivy Day in the Committee Room"; "A Mother"; "Grace"; "The Dead."

Three of these stories were first published in the *Irish Homestead*. See C 29, 30, and 32.

9. DUBLINERS 1916

First American edition; English sheets:

DUBLINERS | BY | JAMES JOYCE | [publisher's emblem] | NEW YORK | B. W. HUEBSCH | 1916

COLLATION: 280 pp. [A]^8, B–R^8, S^4. 18.7 x 12.6 cm., all edges trimmed. Printed on cream-white laid paper; cream-white wove end papers. [A_{2-3}] are cancels, an American title and facing page being substituted for the English; printed on cream-white laid paper watermarked: *Utopian*

PAGINATION: pp.[1–2], blank; p.[3], fly title; p.[4], listing of another work *By the Same Author* ; p.[5], title page; p.[6], blank; p. 7, *Contents* ; p.[8], blank; pp. 9–278, text; pp.[279–80], blank.

BINDING: Blue-green cloth, stamped in green. Front cover: Dubliners | [diagonal rule] | James Joyce Spine: Dubliners | [diagonal rule] | James Joyce | Huebsch Issued in a cream-colored dust wrapper, printed in black.

PUBLICATION DATE AND PRICE: Published after December 15, 1916, and before January 1, 1917. $1.50.

NUMBER OF COPIES: 504 sets of the English sheets were imported by Huebsch from Grant Richards for this edition.

10. DUBLINERS 1917

First American edition; American sheets:

DUBLINERS | BY | JAMES JOYCE | [publisher's emblem] | NEW YORK | B. W. HUEBSCH | 1917

COLLATION: 288 pp. [1–18]^{8}. 18.7 x 12.4 cm., all edges trimmed. Printed on cream-white wove paper; cream-white end papers. In all copies examined pp. 193–288 are printed on an inferior grade of pulp paper.

PAGINATION: p.[1], fly title; p.[2], list of books *By the Same Author* ; p.[3], title page; p.[4], statement of edition and printing, final date: *Second printing, April, 1917* | *Printed in U.S.A.* ; p.[5], *Contents* ; p.[6], blank; pp. 7–288, text.

BINDING: Same as New York 1916 edition. The dust wrapper is also the same as that of the New York 1916 edition, except *Second Printing* is printed in red at the top of the front cover.

PUBLICATION DATE AND PRICE: April 1917. $1.50.

NUMBER OF COPIES: Not ascertained.

NOTES: *Dubliners* was reprinted by Huebsch in January 1922 and February 1925. In November 1926 it was issued in the Modern Library, New York, in an edition of 5,000 copies, with an introduction by Padraic Colum, and has been reprinted twenty-seven times in this series, most recently in April 1950. The total number printed to date is 60,000 copies.

American sheets were used in the second English edition of *Dubliners,* London, Grant Richards, 1918, and in the edition published by the Egoist Press, London, 1922, which carried the erroneous statement that it was the "second edition." The Egoist Press imported 1,000 sets of American sheets for reasons of economy, not because of printing difficulties (letter from Harriet Shaw Weaver, February 25, 1947). There were 168 bound copies and 500 sets of sheets on hand unsold when the Egoist Press disposed of the book to Jonathan Cape in 1924; Cape issued these sheets in two different bindings with no change of the Egoist title page. One of these bindings was orange cloth, the other black cloth. This firm has published all subsequent editions of *Dubliners* in England. *Dubliners* was reset when it was first issued by Cape in the Travellers' Library in 1926 and again when it was first published in Guild Books in 1947. Other Cape editions include Flexibles, 1934, Half Crown Fiction edition, 1936, and Five Shillings edition in 1944. *Dubliners* was reissued in the Travellers' Library in 1950.

Dubliners is included in *The Portable James Joyce* (A 55) and *The Essential James Joyce* (A 56).

In 1932 *Dubliners* was published in a copyright edition by the

Albatross Verlag, Hamburg, Paris, Milan, as Vol. I of the Albatross Modern Continental Library. The edition was issued in yellow and white covers printed in black, printed and bound in Verona by the Stabilimenti A. Mondadori. There was also a special edition of ten copies *hors commerce* printed on Japanese vellum and bound in green half-leather. The author's copy of this special edition is with the Joyce Paris Library at the Lockwood Memorial Library, University of Buffalo.

A discussion of the manuscript corrections to *Dubliners* will be found in the manuscript section of this bibliography (E 2.*j*).

11. A PORTRAIT OF THE ARTIST AS A YOUNG MAN 1916

First edition:

A Portrait of the Artist | as a Young Man | BY | JAMES JOYCE | [publisher's emblem] | NEW YORK | B. W. HUEBSCH | MCMXVI

COLLATION: [iv], 300 pp. [1–19]^8. 18.6 x 12.5 cm., all edges trimmed. Printed on cream-white wove paper; cream-white end papers.

PAGINATION: p. [i], fly title; p. [ii], list of books *By the Same Writer* ; p. [iii], title page; p. [iv], copyright notice and printing statement: *Copyright, 1916, by | B. W. Huebsch | Printed in the United States of America* ; pp. 1–299, text; p.[300], blank.

BINDING: Blue cloth. Front cover, stamped in blind: A Portrait of | the Artist as | a Young Man | [diagonal rule] | James Joyce Spine, gilt stamped: A Portrait of | the Artist as | a Young Man | [diagonal rule] | James Joyce | Huebsch Issued in a cream-colored dust wrapper, printed in black.

PUBLICATION DATE AND PRICE: December 29, 1916. $1.50.

NUMBER OF COPIES: Not ascertained.

NOTES: *A Portrait of the Artist as a Young Man* was reprinted by Huebsch as follows: second, April 1917; third, January or June 1918; fourth, September 1921; fifth, September 1922; sixth, by the Viking Press and B. W. Huebsch, September 1925; seventh, by the Viking Press and B. W. Huebsch, August 1927. In March 1928 it was issued in the Modern Library, New York, in an edition of 8,000 copies, with an introduction by Herbert Gorman, and has been reprinted thirty-seven times in this series, most recently in May 1950, all from the original Huebsch plates. The total number printed to date is 99,000 copies. *A Portrait of the Artist as a Young Man* was reset and published by Signet Books, New York, in March 1948 and reprinted in March 1949, November 1950, and March 1952.

A Portrait of the Artist as a Young Man is included in *The Portable James Joyce* (A 55).

For a record of the serial publication of *A Portrait of the Artist as a Young Man* in the *Egoist* see C 46.

12. A PORTRAIT OF THE ARTIST AS A YOUNG MAN [1917]

First English edition; American sheets:

A Portrait of the Artist | as a Young Man | BY | JAMES JOYCE | THE EGOIST LTD. | OAKLEY HOUSE, BLOOMSBURY STREET, | LONDON

COLLATION: [iv], 300 pp. [1–19]^{8}. 18.1 x 12.3 cm., all edges trimmed. Printed on cream-white wove paper; cream-white end papers.

PAGINATION: p. [i], fly title; p. [ii], list of books *By the Same Writer* ; p. [iii], title page; p. [iv], copyright notice and printing statement: *Copyright, 1916, by* | *B. W. Huebsch* | *Printed in the United States of America* ; pp. 1–299, text; p.[300], blank.

BINDING: Dark green cloth. Front cover, stamped in blind: A PORTRAIT OF THE ARTIST | AS A YOUNG MAN | [rule] | JAMES JOYCE [the foregoing is within a double-rule border] Spine, gilt stamped: [rule] | A | PORTRAIT OF | THE ARTIST AS | A YOUNG MAN | [rule] | JAMES JOYCE | THE EGOIST LTD. | [rule] Issued in a cream-colored dust wrapper, printed in black.

PUBLICATION DATE AND PRICE: February 12, 1917. 6*s.*

NUMBER OF COPIES: "I had not ventured to order more than 750 sets of sheets." Letter from Harriet Shaw Weaver, February 25, 1947.

NOTES: The first edition of *A Portrait of the Artist as a Young Man* was printed in America and the first English edition was made up of American sheets because English printers would not accept the responsibility of printing it (letter from Harriet Shaw Weaver, February 25, 1947). Gorman, 1939, pp. 235–6, quotes the refusals of seven printers, all on moral grounds. Under English law, unlike American, the printing of immoral writings is as actionable as their publication.

13. A PORTRAIT OF THE ARTIST AS A YOUNG MAN [1918]

First English edition; English sheets:

A Portrait of the Artist | as a Young Man | BY | JAMES JOYCE | THE EGOIST LTD. | 23 ADELPHI TERRACE HOUSE, W.C. | LONDON

COLLATION: [vi], 302 pp. [1–18]^8, [19]^{10}. 18.3 x 12.2 cm., all edges trimmed. Printed on cream-white wove paper; cream-white end papers.

PAGINATION: p. [i], fly title; p. [ii], list of books *By the Same Writer* ; p. [iii], title page; p. [iv], copyright notice and printing statement: *Copyright, 1916, by* | *B. W. Huebsch, New York.* | *First edition printed in the United States of America, 1916.* | *Second edition, 1917.* | *"Visiter" Printing Works, Southport.* ; p. [v], quotation from Ovid; p. [vi], blank; pp. 1–299, text; pp. [300–2], blank.

BINDING: Dark green cloth. Front cover, stamped in blind: A PORTRAIT OF THE ARTIST | AS A YOUNG MAN | [rule] | JAMES JOYCE [the foregoing is within a double-rule border] Spine, gilt stamped: [rule] | A | PORTRAIT | OF THE | ARTIST AS | A YOUNG | MAN | JAMES | JOYCE | THE EGOIST LTD. | [rule]

PUBLICATION DATE AND PRICE: March 1918 (see the *Egoist*, London, V.3 [Mar 1918] 47). *4s. 6d.*

NUMBER OF COPIES: 1,000.

NOTES: *A Portrait of the Artist as a Young Man* was published again by the Egoist Press in the spring of 1921 using 1,000 sets of American sheets imported from Huebsch. There were 130 copies of this edition left in 1924 when the Egoist Press disposed of *A Portrait of the Artist as a Young Man* to Jonathan Cape, the firm which has published all subsequent editions of the book in England. Jonathan Cape issued a new edition with type reset in 1924, which was reprinted in 1926 and 1928. The work was issued in the Travellers' Library in 1930 and reprinted five times to 1950; in 1942 in the Five Shillings edition which was reprinted in 1943, 1944, 1945, 1946 (or

1947), and 1948. Other Cape editions include Flexibles, 1934, and Half Crown Fiction, 1936.

A Portrait of the Artist as a Young Man is included in *The Essential James Joyce* (A 56).

In May 1930 *A Portrait of the Artist as a Young Man* was published in a copyright edition by Bernhard Tauchnitz, Leipzig, as Vol. 4937 of Tauchnitz edition, Collection of British and American Authors. The volume was issued in cream-white covers printed in black. In the earliest printing the advertisements in the volume are dated May 1930; subsequent impressions carry advertisements of later dates.

In 1945 *A Portrait of the Artist as a Young Man* was published by the Continental Book Company AB, Stockholm and London, as Vol. 18 of Zephyr Books, A Library of British and American Authors. The volume was issued in blue and white covers printed in pale blue and black.

A discussion of the manuscript corrections to *A Portrait of the Artist as a Young Man* will be found in the manuscript section of this bibliography (E 3.*d*).

14. EXILES 1918

First English edition:

EXILES | A PLAY IN THREE ACTS | BY | JAMES JOYCE | [ornamental leaf] | LONDON | GRANT RICHARDS LTD. | ST. MARTIN'S STREET | 1918

COLLATION: [vi], 158 pp. [A]^8, B–K^8, plus K_2, a folio leaf. 18.5 x 12.3 cm., all edges trimmed. Printed on cream-white wove paper; cream-white end papers.

PAGINATION: p. [i], fly title; p. [ii], list of books *By the Same Writer* and printer: *Printed in Great Britain* | *by* | *Garden City Press Limited* | *Letchworth, Herts.* ; p. [iii], title page; p. [iv], blank; p. [v], characters and setting of the play; p. [vi], blank; pp. 1–158, text.

BINDING: Quarter green cloth, slate green boards. White paper label on front cover: EXILES | *By* | JAMES JOYCE [foregoing is within a single-rule box] Paper label on spine: EXILES | JAMES | JOYCE | [ornament] | GRANT | RICHARDS

PUBLICATION DATE AND PRICE: May 25, 1918. 3*s.* 6*d.*

NUMBER OF COPIES: Not ascertained.

NOTES: The contract for the publication of *Exiles* in the Slocum Library is dated August 31, 1917.

On July 10, 1917, Joyce wrote to John Quinn: "I began to write *Exiles* in the spring of 1914 on notes, and began to draft it in August 1914. I brought the MS with me here [Zurich] from Austria in July, 1915, and finished the play here in September, 1915."

Joyce wrote to Grant Richards on May 3, 1918: ". . . glad to hear *Exiles* is at last ready." And on June 6, 1918: "Thanks for 3 copies of *Exiles*." Joyce also sent to Richards on the latter date corrections which were incorporated in later English editions of *Exiles*. A discussion of these and other manuscript corrections to *Exiles* will be found in the manuscript section of this bibliography (E 4.*c*).

A second English edition of *Exiles* was published by the Egoist Press in 1921 from new type, in an edition of 1,000 copies (500 of them being bound in dark green cloth). There were 168 bound copies and 500 sets of sheets on hand unsold when the Egoist Press disposed of the book to Jonathan Cape in 1924. Cape continued to issue these sheets in a new black cloth binding, with the Egoist dust wrapper. In 1936 Cape issued *Exiles* as New Plays Series No. 6, in a canary yellow cloth binding, stamped in blue. This edition, erroneously advertised as "type entirely re-set," was actually printed from the same plates as the Egoist edition of 1921. *Exiles* was reprinted by Cape in 1950 in a buff cloth binding.

Exiles is included in *The Essential James Joyce* (A 56).

15. EXILES 1918

First American Edition:

EXILES | A PLAY IN THREE ACTS | BY | JAMES JOYCE | [publisher's emblem] | NEW YORK | B. W. HUEBSCH | MCMXVIII

COLLATION: [vi], 154 pp. [1–10]^8. 18.7 x 12.5 cm., all edges trimmed. Printed on cream-white wove paper; cream-white end papers.

PAGINATION: p. [i], fly title; p. [ii], list of books *By the Same Writer* ; p. [iii], title page; p. [iv], copyright notice and printing statement: *Copyright, 1918, by* | *B. W. Huebsch* | *Printed in*

U. S. A. ; p. [v], characters and setting of the play; p. [vi], blank; pp. 1–154, text.

BINDING: Quarter green twill cloth, tan boards, striped vertically. Front cover, stamped in blind: EXILES | [ornamental leaf] | JAMES | JOYCE Spine, gilt stamped: EXILES | [ornament] | JAMES | JOYCE | HUEBSCH Issued in a pale yellow dust wrapper printed in black.

PUBLICATION DATE AND PRICE: May 25, 1918. $1.

NUMBER OF COPIES: Not ascertained.

NOTES: Letter of B. W. Huebsch to Grant Richards, December 10, 1921: "The total sales to October 10, 1921 were 388 copies not enough to earn the advance paid on the book."

Exiles was reissued by Huebsch in 1924. Copies of this reissue have been noted with the tan boards plain and with a vertical herringbone pattern. On November 21, 1945, New Directions, Norfolk, Connecticut, published *Exiles* as No. 13 of the New Classics Series. This edition, for which the Huebsch plates were used, contained an essay on the play by Francis Fergusson.

Exiles is included in *The Portable James Joyce* (A 55).

16. EXILES 1951

JAMES JOYCE | Exiles [in reddish brown] | A PLAY IN THREE ACTS, INCLUDING | HITHERTO UNPUBLISHED NOTES BY | THE AUTHOR, DISCOVERED AFTER HIS | DEATH, AND AN INTRODUCTION | BY PADRAIC COLUM | [publisher's emblem in reddish brown] | THE VIKING PRESS, NEW YORK, 1951

COLLATION: 127, [1] pp. [1–8]^{8}. 23.5 x 15.6 cm., all edges trimmed, top edge stained brown. Printed on cream-white wove paper; end papers reproduce two pages from Joyce's notes.

PAGINATION: p. [1], fly title and statement of limitation: EXILES | [rule] | *This first edition is limited to* | *1900 copies for sale, and 75 copies* | *for private distribution.* ; p. [2], list of books *Also by James Joyce* ; p. [3], title page; p. [4], copyright notice and printing statement: *Copyright 1951 by The Viking Press, Inc.* | *Copyright 1918 by B. W. Huebsch, 1946 by Nora Joyce* | *Published in December 1951* | *Printed in the United States of America* | *by American Book-Stratford Press, Inc., New York* ; p. [5], *Contents* ; p. [6], acknowledgment: *The Notes which follow the play were written by Mr. Joyce in a blue-covered blankbook which is now the property of the University of Buffalo. The publishers acknowledge the gracious cooperation of that institution and of Mr. Charles D. Abbott, its Director of Libraries, as well as of the administrators of the estate of James Joyce.* ; pp. 7–11, *Introduction by Padraic Colum* ; p. [12], blank; p. [13], characters and setting of the play; p. [14], blank; pp. 15–127, text; p. [128], blank.

BINDING: Quarter tan cloth, mauve boards. Spine, stamped in red, reading from top to bottom: *James Joyce* EXILES *Viking* Red and tan striped headband and tailband. Issued in tan dust wrapper printed in reddish brown.

PUBLICATION DATE AND PRICE: December 3, 1951. $5.

NUMBER OF COPIES: 1,975 (1,900 of this limitation).

NOTES: The 75 copies not for sale did not differ from the trade edition of 1,900 copies.

An English edition of this work was published by Jonathan Cape, London, late in 1952.

17. ULYSSES 1922

First edition:

ULYSSES | by | JAMES JOYCE | SHAKESPEARE AND COMPANY | 12, Rue de l'Odéon, 12 | PARIS | 1922

COLLATION: [xii], 740 pp. [*]², [**]⁴, [1]⁸, 2–46⁸, [47]². 23.7 x 18.5 cm., untrimmed and unopened. Printed on white laid paper.

PAGINATION: pp.[i–ii], blank, inserted under folding flaps of outer front cover; pp.[iii–iv], blank; p.[v], fly title; p.[vi], list of books *By the Same Writer* ; p.[vii], title page; p.[viii], copyright notice: . . . *Copyright by James Joyce.* ; p.[ix], limitation notice: *This edition is limited to 1000 copies: | 100 copies (signed) on Dutch | handmade paper numbered from | 1 to 100; 150 copies on vergé | d'Arches numbered from 101 to 250; | 750 copies on handmade paper | numbered from 251 to 1000. | N°* [number stamped in]; p.[x], blank; p.[xi], *The publisher asks the reader's indulgence for typographical errors | unavoidable in the exceptional circumstances. | S. B.* ; p.[xii], blank; p.[1], divisional numeral: I ; p.[2], blank; pp.[3]–50, text of Part I; p.[51], divisional numeral: II ; p.[52], blank; pp.[53]–565, text of Part II; p.[566], blank; p.[567], divisional numeral: III ; p.[568], blank; pp.[569]–732, text of Part III; p.[733], colophon: *Printed | for | Sylvia Beach | by | Maurice Darantière | at | Dijon, France* ; pp.[734–8], blank; pp.[739–40], blank, inserted under folding flaps of outer back cover.

BINDING: Blue paper covers. On front cover in white: ULYSSES | BY | JAMES JOYCE

PUBLICATION DATE AND PRICE: February 2, 1922. 150 fr.

NUMBER OF COPIES: 1,000 (750 on handmade paper).

NOTES: Copies numbered from 101 to 250 are the same as the above except the size is 26.2 x 20.1 cm.; printed on vergé d'Arches paper; price 250 fr. Copies numbered from 1 to 100 are the same except the size is 23.7 x 19.5 cm.; printed on white laid paper watermarked: [device] | VAN GELDER ZONEN ; price 350 fr. Copies 1 to 100 were signed by James Joyce under the limitation notice, p. [ix].

A copy of *Ulysses* (one of 750) with an extra folio leaf (four blank pages) sewn in after $[*]^2$ has been noted.

In an unspecified number of the 750 copies the numbers were erased and rubber stamped "Unnumbered Press Copy," e.g., the Kate Buss copy in the library of T. E. Hanley, the Michael Healy copy in the library of James Laughlin, and the Richard Aldington copy in the Slocum Library. These copies are also stamped "Press Copy" on the fly title and title page.

Ulysses was printed for Shakespeare and Company eleven times. The second and third printings, October 1922 and January 1923, were published for the Egoist Press, London, by John Rodker, Paris, and are described in a separate collation. Subsequent printings were: fourth, January 1924; fifth, September 1924; sixth, August 1925; seventh, October 1925 in the book itself and December 1925 in later notices; eighth, May 1926; ninth, May 1927; tenth, November 1928; eleventh, May 1930.

The fourth, fifth, and sixth printings were issued in white covers with the title and author printed in blue on the front cover and spine. The fourth and fifth were printed on a thick paper of inferior quality and had *Price: Sixty Francs* printed on the back cover. In the fourth, fifth, and sixth printings the text was corrected for the errata which had been issued with the second and third printings, but more typographical errors which had been discovered were listed as *Ulysses | Additional corrections* and included in the regular pagination, pp.[733]–736. The seventh printing, issued in blue covers with title and author in white, also contained these corrections. For the eighth printing of *Ulysses* (text expanded to 735 pages) the type was entirely reset and the "Additional corrections" were, for the most part, incorporated in the text. These plates were used through the eleventh printing. The eighth to eleventh printings were issued in blue covers with title and author in white on front cover and spine.

In a letter to James B. Pinker, July 4, 1931, Sylvia Beach stated that *Ulysses* was then in its 28th thousand and 11th edition. This presumably may be taken for the total number of copies published by her from February 1922 to May 1930.

For a list of the episodes of *Ulysses* published in the *Little Review* and the *Egoist* see C 53 and 54.

18. ULYSSES 1922

First English edition (printed in France):

ULYSSES | by | JAMES JOYCE | PUBLISHED FOR THE | EGOIST PRESS, LONDON | BY JOHN RODKER, PARIS | 1922

COLLATION: [xii], 736 pp. [*]², [**]⁴, [1]⁸, 2–46⁸. 22.6 x 17.5 cm., untrimmed and unopened. Printed on white laid paper.

PAGINATION: pp. [i–ii], blank, inserted under folding flaps of outer front cover; pp. [iii–iv], blank; p. [v], fly title; p. [vi], list of books *By the Same Writer* ; p. [vii], title page; p. [viii], copyright notice: . . . *Copyright by James Joyce.* ; p. [ix], limitation notice: *This edition is limited to | 2000 copies on handmade paper | numbered from 1 to 2000.* | *N°* [number stamped in]; p. [x], statement of edition: *First published by Shakespeare and Company, Paris: February 1922.* | *Published by the Egoist Press, London: October 1922.* ; p. [xi], *The publishers apologize for typographical | errors a list of which is appended.* ; p. [xii], blank; p. [1], divisional numeral: I ; p. [2], blank; pp. [3]–50, text of Part I; p. [51], divisional numeral: II ; p. [52], blank; pp. [53]–565, text of Part II; p. [566], blank; p. [567], divisional numeral: III ; p. [568], blank; pp. [569]–732, text of Part III; p. [733], colophon: *Printed | by | Maurice Darantière | at | Dijon, France* ; p. [734], blank; pp. [735–6], blank, inserted under folding flaps of outer back cover.

BINDING: Blue paper covers. On front cover in white: ULYSSES | BY | JAMES JOYCE

PUBLICATION DATE AND PRICE: October 12, 1922. £2 2s.

NUMBER OF COPIES: 2,000. 500 of these, sent to America, were reported seized and burned by United States government authorities.

NOTES: This edition was printed from the plates of the original edition. Eight pages of "Errata," unopened, listing over two hundred newly discovered typographical errors were laid in.

A letter from Harriet Shaw Weaver, February 25, 1947, states: "A good number of copies sent by ordinary book post to the U.S.A. got through to their various destinations, but some time between October 1922 (when the Egoist edition was published) and December, the U.S.A. censorship authorities evidently became suspicious; copies were held up and accumulated at the U.S.A. post offices until finally 400–500 copies were confiscated and burnt."

It is the conjecture of James F. Spoerri that the statement in the third and subsequent Paris printings of *Ulysses* that 500 copies of this (the first Egoist edition) were destroyed in New York is erroneous. He suggests that these copies were numbered serially from 500 to 1,000 and that if seized they were not destroyed. His reasons for this suggestion are, first, that the only known numbered copy of the third edition (see below) bears the number 827; second, during the past twenty years New York rare-book dealers have had numerous copies of this edition, in new condition, numbered between 500 and 1,000.

A request for information concerning the destruction of these 500 copies addressed to the Collector of Customs at New York has failed to produce an answer.

In late January 1923 John Rodker published a second English edition of *Ulysses* in Paris. This volume is exactly the same as the first English edition, except for the limitation notice, p. [ix], which reads: *This edition of 500 copies is | specially reprinted to replace | those destroyed in transit | to the U. S. A. | N°* . It is stated in later printings of *Ulysses* that of these 500 copies, 499 were seized and confiscated by the English customs authorities at Folkestone. At least three copies, however, have survived. There are two in the Slocum Library, the Rodker copy (unnumbered) and the Keynes copy presented by Joyce to Mike and Maggy Strator, March 13, 1924 (numbered in ink 827), and a third (unnumbered) in the James Joyce Paris Library, now at the Lockwood Memorial Library, University of Buffalo.

19. ULYSSES [1929]

First American edition (unauthorized):

ULYSSES | by | JAMES JOYCE | SHAKESPEARE AND COMPANY | 12, RUE DE L'ODÉON, 12 | PARIS | 1927

COLLATION: [viii], 736 pp. [1]^{4}, [2–24]^{16}. 21.9 x 16 cm., untrimmed and unopened. Printed on white wove paper.

PAGINATION: pp.[i–ii], blank; p.[iii], divisional numeral: I (misplaced; reversed with fly title); p.[iv], blank; p.[v], title page; p.[vi], copyright notice: . . . *Copyright by James Joyce* ; p.[vii], printing history of *Ulysses*, same as in legitimate ninth edition but with variations in type and punctuation; p.[viii], blank; p.[1], fly title (misplaced; reversed with divisional numeral: I); p.[2], list of books *By the Same Writer* , giving a publisher of these books incorrectly as "Jonthan Cape" instead of "Jonathan Cape"; pp.[3]–50, text of Part I; p.[51], divisional numeral: II ; p.[52], blank; pp.[53]–570, text of Part II; p.[571], divisional numeral: III ; p.[572], blank; pp. [573]–735, text of Part III; p.[736], blank.

BINDING: Blue wrappers, printed in white. Front cover: ULYSSES | BY | JAMES JOYCE The wrappers do not have folding flaps as in the legitimate edition.

PUBLICATION DATE AND PRICE: 1929. Price not ascertained; copies were sold by the publisher to the book trade for $5, and the dealer usually set his own price. John J. Slocum purchased a copy in 1930 for $15.

NUMBER OF COPIES: *c.*2,000–3,000.

NOTES: This pirated edition of *Ulysses* is discussed at some length by R. F. Roberts in his pioneer article, "Bibliographical Notes on James Joyce's 'Ulysses'," in the *Colophon*, New York, N.S. 1.4 (Spring, 1936) 565–79.

Among the many points in which this piracy differs from the legitimate ninth printing are the misprint "Jonthan" for "Jonathan" (p.[2]), the reversal of the position of the fly title and divisional numeral I, the absence of title and author on the spine, and a very large number of typographical errors. On p. 323 of this piracy, for example, l. 29 of the legitimate edition is inverted and inserted as the third line from the bottom. Roberts also states that "The pagination is the same but the type font is perceptibly smaller; the paper is a considerably heavier stock and the book is consequently about one-eighth of an inch thicker." This edition is not a copy of the photographic reproduction mentioned by Joyce in his letter to Bennett A. Cerf, April 2, 1932, printed in the 1934 Random House edition of *Ulysses* (A 21), but a piracy from new plates. The photographic reproduction mentioned by Joyce almost certainly never existed.

Copies of this pirated ninth edition reached Paris and were imported into the United States as genuine copies. One of these, sent by Joyce to Bennett A. Cerf of Random House, was used in setting up the first authorized American edition of *Ulysses.*

This pirated edition of the ninth Shakespeare and Company *Ulysses* was printed by Adolph and Rudolph Loewinger, 230 West 17th St., New York, for Samuel Roth, publisher of *Two Worlds* and *Two Worlds Monthly*, and his brother Max Roth. It was unauthorized by Joyce and sold illegally in the United States. Many copies of this piracy were seized by the Society for the Suppression of Vice on October 5, 1929.

For a record of Roth's publication of *Ulysses* in *Two Worlds Monthly* see C 68.

20. ULYSSES 1932

ULYSSES | *by* | JAMES JOYCE | *VOLUME ONE* [*TWO*] | THE ODYSSEY PRESS | HAMBURG [dot] PARIS [dot] BOLOGNA

COLLATION: 2 vols. Vol. I: [1]–[400], [iv] pp.; Vol. II: [iv], 401–[796] pp. Vol. I: [43,1]^8, 43,2–43,25^8, 2 unsigned leaves; Vol. II: 2 unsigned leaves, 43,26–43,49^8, 43,50^4, 2 unsigned leaves. 18 x 11.1 cm., all edges trimmed. Printed on white wove paper.

PAGINATION: Vol. I: p.[1], fly title; p.[2], blank; p.[3], title page; p.[4], printing history of *Ulysses*, including: *First issued by The Odyssey Press: December 1932.* | [star] | *The present edition may be regarded as the* | *definitive standard edition, as it has been* | *specially revised, at the author's request, by* | *Stuart Gilbert.* and copyright notice: *Copyright 1932* | *By The Odyssey Press, Christian Wegner, Hamburg* | *Imprimé en Allemagne* ; pp. 5–[400], text of Vol. I; p.[i], blank; p.[ii], colophon: *This edition is composed in* | *Baskerville type cut by the* | *Monotype Corporation. The* | *paper is made by the Papier-* | *fabrik Bautzen. The printing and* | *the binding are the work of* | *Oscar Brandstetter* [dot] *Abteilung* | *Jakob Hegner* [dot] *Leipzig* ; pp.[iii–iv], blank.

Vol. II: p.[i], fly title; p.[ii], blank; p.[iii], title page; p.[iv], copyright notice; pp. 401–[792], text of Vol. II; p.[793], blank; p.[794], colophon as in Vol. I; pp. [795–6], blank.

BINDING: Stiff gray paper covers, printed in reddish brown. Front cover: ULYSSES | BY | JAMES JOYCE | [decorative rule] Spine: ULYSSES | BY | JAMES | JOYCE | I [II] | THE | ODYSSEY | PRESS Back cover: IN TWO VOLUMES | RM 5.60 [rule] FRS 36.00 [rule] LIRE 28.00 | NOT TO BE INTRODUCED INTO THE BRITISH EMPIRE OR THE U.S.A. Issued in transparent tissue protective wrappers in plain cardboard box.

PUBLICATION DATE AND PRICE: December 1, 1932. RM 5.60. 36 fr. L.28.

NUMBER OF COPIES: Not ascertained.

NOTES: The inner front covers of both volumes contain signed critical comments on *Ulysses*.

The Odyssey Press *Ulysses* was also published in a one-volume thin-paper edition in December 1932 (number of copies not ascertained) and shortly after in a special two-volume edition. The special edition is slightly taller than the regular and has an extra leaf tipped in before the fly title of Vol. I which reads: *Of the present special edition,* | *thirty-five copies, of which twen-* | *ty-five only are for sale, were* | *printed upon hand-made paper* | *and signed by the author.* | *This copy was printed* | *for* | [recipient's name printed in] | [signature of James Joyce]. The Stuart Gilbert copy and the James Joyce copy are bound in three-quarters blue morocco with marbled paper sides, top edge gilt. The Harriet Shaw Weaver copy and the Giorgio Joyce copy are bound in the regular gray paper covers.

The Odyssey Press edition of *Ulysses* was reprinted as follows: second impression, October 1933; third impression, August 1935; fourth impression, April 1939.

This edition, revised by Stuart Gilbert at the request of Joyce, is generally considered to be the most accurate and authoritative text of *Ulysses*. The first edition contains a number of typographical errors, most of which were corrected in later impressions.

It has been reported that the plates of the Odyssey Press edition of *Ulysses* were destroyed in the bombing of Hamburg during World War II.

21. ULYSSES 1934

First authorized American edition:

[double title page, verso:] U [recto:] JAMES | JOYCE | LYSSES [Note: In the foregoing the U on verso extends the height and width of the type page.]

COLLATION: xviii, 774 pp. [1–24][16] [25][12]. 20.7 x 13.9 cm., top edge stained brown, other edges trimmed. Printed on white wove paper; cream-colored end papers.

PAGINATION: p.[i], blank; pp.[ii–iii], double title page; p.[iv], blank; p.[v], [publisher's emblem], copyright notice, and printer: *Ulysses by James Joyce | First American edition, published by Random | House, New York, 1934. Copyright, 1918, 1919, | 1920, by Margaret Caroline Anderson. Copy- | right, 1934, by the Modern Library, Inc. | Printed and bound in the U. S. A. by H. Wolff, | New York City. Designed by Ernst Reichl.* ; p.[vi], blank; pp. vii–viii, *Foreword* by Morris L. Ernst dated December 11, 1933; pp. ix–xiv, text of the decision by Hon. John M. Woolsey lifting the ban on *Ulysses,* dated December 6, 1933; pp. xv–xvii, letter, dated April 2, 1932, from Joyce to Bennett A. Cerf; p.[xviii], blank; p.[1], half-title; p.[2], blank; p.[3], divisional numeral: I ; pp. [4]–51, text of Part I; p.[52], blank; p.[53], divisional numeral: II ; pp. [54]–593, text of Part II; p.[594], blank; p.[595], divisional numeral: III ; pp. [596]–[768], text of Part III; pp. [769–74], blank.

BINDING: Cream-colored cloth, stamped in black and red; beveled edges. Front cover: JAMES | JOYCE | ULYSSES [in red] Spine: JAMES | JOYCE | ULYS [in red] | SES [in red] | RANDOM HOUSE Issued in cream-colored dust wrapper, printed in black and red.

PUBLICATION DATE AND PRICE: January 25, 1934. $3.50.

NUMBER OF COPIES: 100 (first printing for reasons of copyright); 10,300 (second printing).

NOTES: As R. F. Roberts points out in his article cited in the notes to the unauthorized first American edition of *Ulysses* (A 19), this Random House edition was set up from the text of a copy of that edition, incorporating most of its typographical errors and adding a few new ones. Some of the errors were corrected in later printings and editions.

The circumstances of the trial of *Ulysses*, the decision of the court, and the speedy publication of the book are described in "Publishing 'Ulysses' " by Bennett Cerf in *Contempo*, Chapel Hill, N.C., III.13 (Feb 15, 1934) 1–2, and in Gorman, 1939, pp. 316–23.

Ten printings of the Random House edition, the last in 1939, totaled 50,625 copies. The plates were used in the Modern Library Giant edition published in September 1940 in an edition of 10,000 copies. This edition has been reprinted fifteen times, most recently in June 1950, for a total of 137,000 copies.

On May 10, 1949, *Ulysses* was reissued by Random House. 3,700 copies were printed from the original plates with a new binding and dust-wrapper design by E. McKnight Kauffer.

22. ULYSSES 1935

Ulysses [in script] | by James Joyce | [ornament] | WITH AN INTRODUCTION BY STUART GILBERT AND ILLUSTRATIONS BY | Henri Matisse | THE LIMITED EDITIONS CLUB | *New York, 1935*

COLLATION: xviii, 370 pp. [1–24]^8, with tipped-in leaves after [1]$_8$ and [23]$_6$. 29.6 x 23 cm., top edge sprinkled brown, other edges untrimmed. Printed on cream-white toned Worthy rag paper. Cream-white end papers.

PAGINATION: pp. [i–ii], blank; p. [iii], title page; p. [iv], copyright notice: *The text of "Ulysses" is copyright 1934 by Random House, Inc.* | *The special contents of this edition are copyright 1935 by* | *The Limited Editions Club, Inc.* ; pp. v–[xvi], *Introduction* by Stuart Gilbert; p. [xvii], half-title and contents; p. [xviii], blank; pp. 1–363, text; p. [364], blank; p. [365], colophon: *This edition of James Joyce's Ulysses* | *consists of fifteen hundred copies* | *made for the members of* | *The Limited Editions Club* | *The illustrative etchings and drawings* | *having been created especially* | *for this edition by* | *Henri Matisse* | *The edition was designed by George Macy* | *and printed at The Printing-Office of* | *The Limited Editions Club, this copy being* | *number* [number written in ink] | *signed by* [Henri Matisse] | [James Joyce]; pp. [366–70], blank.

BINDING: Brown Bancroft buckram, gilt stamped. Front cover design by LeRoy H. Appleton, gilt stamped and embossed in bas-relief. Spine embossed and stamped: [ornament] | *Ulysses* | [ornament] | BY | JAMES | JOYCE | [ornament] | ILLUSTRATED | BY | HENRI | MA-

TISSE | THE | LIMITED | EDITIONS | CLUB | [ornament] Issued in transparent tissue protective wrapper, boxed.

PUBLICATION DATE AND PRICE: October 22, 1935. $10 to members of the Limited Editions Club; copies signed by Joyce were sold to members for $15.

NUMBER OF COPIES: 1,500; only 250 were signed by Joyce.

NOTES: The text of *Ulysses* is printed in double columns throughout; the running title and pagination are printed in brown. The six etchings by Henri Matisse with their accompanying sketches on yellow and blue paper depict the Calypso, Aeolus, Cyclops, Nausicaa, Circe, and Ithaca episodes. These six etchings were issued separately by the Print Club, New York, 1935, in an edition of 150 copies.

The text of this edition is based on that of the Odyssey Press edition (A 20), second impression, and is therefore the most accurate text of *Ulysses* that has been published in the United States. A full description of the production of this edition appears in the *Monthly Letter of the Limited Editions Club*, 77 (Oct 1935).

23. ULYSSES 1936

First English edition (printed in England):

ULYSSES | *James Joyce* | JOHN LANE THE BODLEY HEAD | BURY STREET WCI | LONDON

COLLATION: xvi, 768 pp. [A]^8, B–3C^8. 25.7 x 19 cm., top edge gilt, other edges untrimmed. Printed on Japon Vellum paper. Japon Vellum end papers.

PAGINATION: pp. [i–iv], blank; p. [v], fly title; p. [vi], blank; p. [vii], title page; p. [viii], blank; p. [ix], limitation notice: *This edition published 1936 | Limited to 1,000 copies, | divided as follows: | 100 copies on mould-made paper bound in | calf vellum and signed by the author | 900 copies on Japon Vellum paper bound in | linen buckram, unsigned | This is number* [number written in ink]; p. [x], printer: *Made in Great Britain | Printed by Western Printing Services Ltd, Bristol | on paper supplied by Spalding and Hodge Ltd | and bound by | the Leighton Straker Bookbinding Co.* | [star]; p. xi, list of *Previous Editions of Ulysses* ; p. [xii], blank; p. xiii, contents; p. [xiv], blank; p. [xv], half-title; p. [xvi], blank; pp. 1–742, text; pp.

743–7, *Appendix A. International Protest and Injunction against Samuel Roth* ; pp. 747–64, *Appendix B.* , letter from Joyce to Bennett A. Cerf dated April 2, 1932; text of the decision by Hon. John M. Woolsey lifting the ban on *Ulysses* dated December 6, 1933; decision of the United States Court of Appeals rendered August 7, 1934; foreword to the first American edition by Morris L. Ernst; pp. 765–[766], *Appendix C. Bibliography of Works by Mr. James Joyce.* ; pp. [767–8], blank.

BINDING: Green linen buckram, gilt stamped. Front cover: Homeric bow, 23 cm. in height. Spine: ULYSSES | James Joyce | THE BODLEY HEAD Green and yellow striped headband. Issued in tan dust wrapper, printed in black, with Homeric bow on spine, printed in red. The binding and the Homeric bow were designed by Eric Gill.

PUBLICATION DATE AND PRICE: October 3, 1936. £3 3*s*.

NUMBER OF COPIES: 1,000 (900 of this issue).

NOTES: In copies 1–100 the title page, with the exception of the author's name, is printed in blue. These copies are printed on mold-made paper. On p. [ix] *This copy is No.* below the limitation notice is printed instead of written in ink; the number, however, is added in ink, and Joyce's signature appears directly below. Copies 1–100 are bound in cream-colored calf vellum, gilt stamped. The Homeric bow appears on the front and back covers and the title and author on the spine, but the publisher's name is omitted. There is a blue and white striped headband and tailband. These copies were issued in a decorated box with a blue-green label and were priced at £6 6*s*.

The text of this edition is based on that of the Odyssey Press edition (A20), second impression, but at least two dozen new typographical errors have been noted which have not been corrected in later John Lane editions.

The bibliography, containing a number of inaccuracies, was prepared by Peter Pertzoff, then a graduate student at Harvard University. Pertzoff submitted the bibliography to Joyce, but it was neither acknowledged nor returned. Joyce's associate Paul Léon sent the bibliography to John Lane, apparently to fulfill a request from them for a bibliography for this edition. Pertzoff was not aware that the bibliography was being used until he saw it in print. The contemporary reprints of *Ibsen's New Drama* and *James Clarence Mangan* listed in the published bibliography were inserted through a printer's error and were not in Pertzoff's original bibliography. Some other inaccuracies such as the title of Sheehy-Skeffington's essay have been corrected in later John Lane printings of *Ulysses.*

The John Lane *Ulysses* was issued in a trade edition in September 1937, reproduced from the original by photo-offset but reduced in size. This was reprinted in 1941, 1947 (in Holland), and 1949.

24. POMES PENYEACH 1927

First edition:

POMES PENYEACH | BY | JAMES JOYCE | SHAKESPEARE AND COMPANY | PARIS | 1927

COLLATION: [24] pp. A single unsigned quire of 12 leaves. 11.9 x 9.3 cm., all edges trimmed. Printed on cream-white wove paper.

PAGINATION: p.[1], blank; p.[2], copyright notice: *Copyright by James Joyce | 1927* ; p.[3], fly title; p.[4], list of works *By the Same Writer* ; p.[5], title page; p.[6], blank; pp.[7–21], text; p.[22], colophon: *Of these Pomes thirteen | copies have been printed | on Dutch hand-made paper | and numbered 1 to 13.* ; pp.[23–4], blank. An errata slip of three lines has been tipped in facing the colophon on p.[22].

BINDING: Pale green boards, printed in dark green. Front cover: POMES PENYEACH | by | JAMES JOYCE Spine blank. Back cover: PRICE ONE SHILLING | Herbert Clarke, Paris

PUBLICATION DATE AND PRICE: July 5, 1927. 1*s.*, or 12 fr.

NUMBER OF COPIES: Not ascertained.

NOTES: Pomes Penyeach contains thirteen poems. Beneath each poem the place and year of composition are given in italics.

The first edition of *Pomes Penyeach* was preceded by two trial printings. Of these there were three copies of each printed, according to the Ulysses Bookshop Catalogue, New York, 1933, p. 27; half a dozen copies of the first, according to the Shakespeare and Company Catalogue, Paris, 1935, No. 16.

Of the first trial printing Sylvia Beach owns a copy, and there are two copies, the Tenney and the Esher-Keynes, in the Slocum Library. These have pale green paper covers, printed in dark green. On the front cover the letters in *Pomes Penyeach* measure 3 mm. in height and the distance from the initial *P* to the final *H* is 5.3 cm.; in the first edition and the second trial printing the letters are 4 mm. in height and the distance from the initial *P* to the final *H* is 6.7 cm. The copies in the Slocum Library differ as follows: The Tenney copy measures 11.9 x 8.7 cm. and is stapled once through the center fold. The Esher-Keynes copy measures 11.7 x 8.7 cm. and is sewn through the center fold. On the verso of the title page of the latter copy Joyce has written in ink: "*Italics* | Copyright by James Joyce | in the United States | of America"; he also indicated proposed changes in the colophon which were not carried out. This first trial printing contains twenty pages; pp.[1–2] and [23–4] in the above collation were added in the second trial printing. The back cover reads: PRICE ONE SHILLING | Herbert Clarke | Paris.

The second trial printing is the same as the published edition, except that the back cover is blank and there is no errata slip. The Tenney and Esher-Keynes copies of the second trial printing are also in the Slocum Library.

The thirteen copies on Dutch handmade paper were probably all reserved for presentation. They measure 12.7 x 13.2 cm., untrimmed and unopened, and are printed on white laid paper watermarked: VAN GELDER ZONEN The number is stamped in below the colophon. The binding is similar to that of the regular first edition, except that it is of larger size to enclose the larger leaf. Two of these thirteen copies, which are in the Slocum Library, were presented by Joyce to Sylvia Beach (No. 1) and Claud Sykes (No. 13). There are also copies in the libraries of Constantine P. Curran and Harriet Shaw Weaver.

The name of the printer on the back cover, Herbert Clarke, is believed to be a pseudonym of the American poet Harry Crosby.

For poems from *Pomes Penyeach* first published in periodicals see C 43, 48, 51, 55, 56, and 57.

25. POMES PENYEACH 1931

First authorized American edition:

POMES PENYEACH | BY | JAMES JOYCE | SYLVIA BEACH | 1931

COLLATION: [20] pp. A single unsigned quire of 10 leaves. 12.2 x 9.3 cm., all edges trimmed. Printed on cream-white wove paper.

PAGINATION: p.[1], fly title; p.[2], list of books *By the Same Writer* ; p.[3], title page; p.[4], copyright notice: *Copyright 1931 by Sylvia Beach* | *Printed in the U. S. A.* ; pp.[5–19], text; p.[20], blank.

BINDING: Gray paper covers, printed in black. Front cover: POMES PENYEACH | BY | JAMES JOYCE

PUBLICATION DATE AND PRICE: May 2, 1931. Not for sale.

NUMBER OF COPIES: 50, according to Princeton University Press records.

NOTES: These copies were printed by the Princeton University Press, Princeton, New Jersey, for Sylvia Beach of Paris solely to copyright the work in the United States.

The errata of the Paris first edition are corrected in the text of this edition.

Copies of this edition are in the Princeton University Library and the Slocum Library.

26. POMES PENYEACH 1931

POMES PENYEACH [in red] | BY | JAMES JOYCE | PRIVATELY PRINTED | CLEVELAND | 1931

COLLATION: [28] pp. A single unsigned quire of 14 leaves. 17.7 x 12.9 cm., top and bottom edges trimmed, fore edge untrimmed. Printed on white Georgian Book laid paper watermarked: Georgian . End papers same as book stock.

PAGINATION: pp.[1–3], blank; p.[4], copyright notice: *Copyright by James Joyce* | *1927* ; p.[5], fly title; p.[6], list of books *By the Same Author*, including *Work in Progress* ; p.[7], title page; p.[8], blank; pp.[9–22], text; p.[23], blank; p.[24], limitation notice: *This edition of Pomes Penyeach* | *is limited to one hundred copies* | *printed by hand on Georgian* | *Book paper and numbered one* | *to one hundred.* [number inserted in ink]; pp.[25–8], blank.

BINDING: Dark brown cloth, gilt stamped. Front cover: POMES PENYEACH | [rule] | JAMES JOYCE

PUBLICATION DATE AND PRICE: Probably September 1931. One of the printers recalls that the book was bound "in approximately April 1931," but records of the National Library Bindery of East Cleveland show that the first bill for binding charges on *Pomes Penyeach* was sent out on September 21, 1931. It is improbable, therefore, that this Cleveland edition preceded the first authorized American edition published May 2, 1931.

Most of the copies were given away, but a few—not more than 20—were sold at about $1 each.

NUMBER OF COPIES: 103, of which 100 were numbered.

NOTES: This edition was the work of two young men in Cleveland, Ohio, Alexander H. Buchman and Edwin A. Johnson. Buchman has written James F. Spoerri as follows:

It is my recollection that 103 copies were printed of which 100 were numbered. The paper was Georgian Book; the type-face I have forgotten; the book was hand-set of course (by myself mainly), and the printing took about three months of catch-as-catch-can efforts. All copies were bound in brown buckram by a local (East Cleveland) bindery in approximately April, 1931. The text was filched from a small paper-bound green volume published by . . . Faber & Faber of London. My brother (then in Paris) sent it to me along with I believe, "Ulysses."

Since the Faber & Faber edition was not published until 1933, Buchman almost certainly used the Shakespeare and Company Paris edition and corrected the textual errors according to the errata slip.

Buchman's letter continues:

We thought it might be a worthwhile effort to print "Pomes," since there was no American edition we knew of, and since we assumed that Miss Beach would readily grant permission for an edition of 100 copies. After the book was printed, we were told emphatically by Miss Beach in a letter from 12 Rue de l'Odéon that we would be beheaded, or such, if we dared to print "Pomes." Since "Pomes" had already been printed, we had little choice but to destroy the books or give them away. We chose the latter, though if my memory is correct, we sold about 20 copies—no more—for about $1.00 each.

The preceding item (the Princeton edition) was evidently the direct outcome of the letter to Miss Beach.

In at least one other book printed by Buchman and Johnson the imprint of the White Horse Press was used.

The compilers are grateful to R. F. Roberts for his help in preparing this collation, and to James F. Spoerri for his assistance in locating copies of the work.

27. POMES PENYEACH 1932

First English edition (printed in France):

Pomes Penyeach | by | James Joyce | Initial | Letters Designed and

Illuminated by | Lucia Joyce | The Obelisk Press | Paris | Desmond Harmsworth Ltd | London | 1932 | [ornament]
[Note: the foregoing is in facsimile of the handwriting of James Joyce; the ornament (approximately 9 x 9.9 cm.) occupies the lower right-hand corner of the title page.]

COLLATION: [36] pp. Nine folio leaves, folded and laid loosely one within another. 25.5 x 33 cm., all edges untrimmed. Entire text in facsimile of the handwriting of James Joyce, with colored initial at the beginning of each poem. Transparent tissue, containing printed text of the poem in green in lower left-hand corner, laid in before each page of text. Printed on Japan nacre paper.

PAGINATION: pp.[1–3], blank; p.[4], number and signature by Joyce in MS: "No 4 | James Joyce" [Slocum Library copy]; p.[5], title page; p.[6], blank; pp.[7–32], text, on recto of each leaf, verso remaining blank; p.[33], limitation notice: *This edition is limited to | twenty five copies, all on Japan | nacre, numbered 1–25 and | signed by | James Joyce* ; p.[34], printer: [in small green type at the lower right-hand corner of the page] *Imprimerie Vendome | Marcel Servant | 338 Rue Saint-Honoré | Paris* ; pp.[35–6], blank.

BINDING: Enclosed in portfolio of green watered silk over boards with folding flaps and green ribbon ties. Front cover, gilt stamped in facsimile of Joyce's handwriting: Pomes Penyeach | by | James Joyce

PUBLICATION DATE AND PRICE: October 1932. 1,000 fr. On October 28, 1932, Paul Léon, Paris, wrote James Pinker in London that 10 copies of this edition of *Pomes Penyeach* were being held by French customs authorities, who claimed great sums for the silk case.

NUMBER OF COPIES: 25, plus an unspecified number of copies *hors commerce.*

28. POMES PENYEACH 1933

First English edition (printed in England):

Pomes | Penyeach | by | James | Joyce | London | Faber & Faber | 24 Russell Square

COLLATION: 24 pp. A single unsigned quire of 12 leaves. 18.5 x 12.3 cm., all edges trimmed. Printed on cream-white wove paper.

PAGINATION: pp.[1–2], blank; p.[3], fly title; p.[4], list of books

By the same writer ; p.[5], title page; p.[6], printing history and printer: *First published, July mcmxxvii | by Shakespeare & Co., Paris | First issued in this edition | March mcmxxxiii | by Faber and Faber Limited | 24 Russell Square London, W.C. | Printed in Great Britain by | R. MacLehose and Company Limited | The University Press Glasgow | All rights reserved* ; p. 7, *Contents* ; p.[8], blank; pp. 9–22, text; pp.[23–4], blank.

BINDING: Plain white stiff paper, covered by a pale blue-gray cover, which is included in the sewing of the gathering. Tied through the center fold with pale blue-gray thread. Outer front cover printed the same as the title page. On front end flap, the price: *1 / – | net* ; back end flap blank. Covers in other colors have been noted.

PUBLICATION DATE AND PRICE: March 16, 1933. 1*s*. The British Museum copy was received March 2, 1933.

NUMBER OF COPIES: Not ascertained for the first edition. 7,623 copies of all printings had been sold to May 31, 1948.

NOTES: Reprinted March 1933, February 1939, July 1942, May or June 1945, and March 1949. Reprints issued in different colored covers and with different colored threads.

Pomes Penyeach is included in *The Essential James Joyce* (A 56).

29. THE JOYCE BOOK [1933]

THE JOYCE BOOK | [ornament] | THE SYLVAN PRESS | AND HUMPHREY MILFORD | OXFORD UNIVERSITY PRESS | AMEN HOUSE, WARWICK SQUARE | LONDON, E.C.4

COLLATION: 88 pp. [1–11]^{4}. 34.5 x 25.5 cm., top edge silver, other edges untrimmed. Printed on grayish white mold-made paper. Grayish white end papers.

PAGINATION: p.[1], fly title; p.[2], blank; p.[3], title page; p. [4], printing statement: *Printed in Great Britain* ; p.[5], portrait of Joyce by Augustus John in collotype reproduction; p.[6], blank; p.[7], *Contents* ; p.[8], blank; p.[9], *Editor's Note* by *Herbert Hughes* ; p.[10], blank; p.[11], *Prologue by James Stephens* [poem]; p.[12], blank; pp. 13–15, *James Joyce as Poet* by *Padraic Colum* ; pp.[16]–77, text of poems and music, each poem printed on the verso of a leaf and immediately followed by the text set to music, each by a different composer; p.[78], blank; pp. 79–[84], *Epilogue* by *Arthur Symons* ; p.[85], colophon: *The Joyce Book was designed by Hu-*

bert Foss and | set, engraved, and printed in England by Henderson | & Spalding Ltd., at the Sylvan Press, Sylvan Grove, | London, S.E.15. The type used throughout is Mono- | type Goudy Modern, and for engraving the words | under the music, special punches were cut by the | Monotype Corporation Ltd. The paper was mould- | made in Holland and the binding is of hand-woven | silk from Edinburgh Weavers. The collotype | frontispiece was printed by John Johnson, at the | University Press, Oxford. Five hundred copies were | printed, of which only four hundred and fifty are | for sale. | This is number | [number written in ink]; pp.[86–8], blank.

BINDING: Dark blue silk over boards, stamped in silver. Another copy, gilt stamped, is in the Slocum Library. Front cover: the | Joyce | book Blue and white striped headband. Issued in a blue-gray envelope, printed in dark blue on front: the | Joyce | book

PUBLICATION DATE AND PRICE: March 1933. 42*s*. The British Museum copy was received on February 18, 1933.

NUMBER OF COPIES: 500, 450 of which were for sale.

NOTES: Musical settings of the poems in *Pomes Penyeach* (A 24). A list of the composers and the poem which each set to music will be found in the music section of this bibliography (F 15).

30. WORK IN PROGRESS VOLUME I 1928

First edition:

JAMES JOYCE | WORK IN PROGRESS | VOLUME | I | NEW YORK [dot] DONALD FRIEDE [dot] MCMXXVII

COLLATION: [ii], 106 pp. [1–6]^8, [7]^6. 29.2 x 19.8 cm., all edges trimmed. Printed on cream-white wove paper; cream-white end papers.

PAGINATION: pp.[i–ii], blank; p.[1], fly title; p.[2], blank; p.[3], title page; p.[4], copyright notice and statement of printing: *Copyright, 1928, by Donald Friede. Printed in U. S. A. | Typography by S. A. Jacobs* ; p.[5], half-title; p.[6], blank; pp. 7–100, text; pp.[101–6], blank.

BINDING: Black cloth, gilt stamped. Front cover: JAMES JOYCE | WORK IN PROGRESS | VOLUME | I Spine, reading from top to bottom: JAMES JOYCE [dot] WORK IN PROGRESS [dot] VOLUME I

PUBLICATION DATE AND PRICE: January 9, 1928. Not for sale.

NUMBER OF COPIES: 20.

NOTES: "In connection with my edition of *Work in Progress*, 15 copies only were printed for copyright purposes, all of them identically bound. The publication date was in early January, 1928. The reason that the title-page reads 1927 was that the book was set up in 1927 and we neglected to change the title-page before printing." Letter from Donald Friede, June 30, 1938.

". . . it was pretty much at Elliot Paul's request that I undertook to print, at my own expense, no more than twenty copies of an edition of certain parts of *Work in Progress*, setting up this material from copies of *transition*. I say no more than twenty copies because I know that some sixteen copies were given away by me to various people associated with me at Boni & Liveright." Letter from Donald Friede, April 2, 1950.

A further account of the publication of this book appears in Friede's book *The Mechanical Angel*, New York, Alfred A. Knopf, 1948, pp. 70–3.

On February 17, 1928, Friede assigned the copyright on *Work in Progress Volume I*, which had been in his name, to James Joyce.

CONTENTS: A reprint of Part 1 of *Finnegans Wake* as it appeared in *transition*, Paris, April–November, 1927 (FW 3-216).

31. WORK IN PROGRESS PART 11 AND 12 [1928]

[ornamental border] | [light rule] | [heavy rule] | JAMES JOYCE | [rule] | Work in Progress | Part 11 and 12 | [heavy rule] | [light rule] | [ornamental border]

[Note: The foregoing appears on the front cover, which is used as the title page.]

COLLATION: 40 pp. A single unsigned quire of 10 folio leaves, stapled. 19.6 x 13.9 cm., all edges trimmed. Printed on cream-white wove paper.

PAGINATION: pp. 1–12, text, with heading on p. 1: *Continuation of a Work | in Progress*[1] *| by James Joyce* . Footnote (1) refers to previous publication of this and other portions in *transition;* pp. 13–35, text, with heading on p. 13: *Continuation of a Work | in Prog-*

ress[1] | *by James Joyce* . This footnote also refers to previous publications in *transition;* pp.[36–40], blank.

BINDING: Orange covers, stapled. Front cover, serving as title page, printed as above.

PUBLICATION DATE AND PRICE: July 24, 1928. Printed for copyright purposes and not for sale.

NUMBER OF COPIES: 5.

NOTES: No notice of copyright appears in this work. The text of Part 11 originally printed in *transition*, Paris, 11 (Feb 1928), appears as FW 282–304. The text of Part 12 originally printed in *transition*, Paris, 12 (Mar 1928), appears as FW 403–28.

This fragment was printed for copyright purposes only to prevent further piracy of *Work in Progress* in *Two Worlds* (C 65) by Samuel Roth. Joyce's Paris attorney wrote to his New York partners February 22, 1928: "There is some dispute about the copyrights and Joyce wishes to get the first pages published in America to comply with copyright law. He will need three copies, two for the copyright office and one for himself. It would of course be well to have a few more copies struck off if once the thing is set up."

On July 9, 1928, the first letter of the New York law firm to the printer Paul Maisel and Company set the conditions under which the publication was to take place:

> There are sent to you with this the February and March 1928 editions of "Transition," each of which includes an installment of New Work by James Joyce. It is our desire to have these two installments printed and bound together in one volume in such a manner as to be acceptable to the Copyright office at Washington. We presume you know the proper form to do this. We should like to emphasize that we desire only five (5) copies to be made.

Of the five copies ordered, two were sent to a Washington attorney for transmittal to the Copyright Office on July 21, 1928. These two copies were received by the Copyright Office August 6, 1928, and copyright issued as of July 24, 1928.

Three copies of *Work in Progress Part 11 and 12* have been located in the James Joyce Paris Library now at the Lockwood Memorial Library, University of Buffalo; the Library of Congress; and the Slocum Library.

Maurice Bernstien of Paul Maisel and Company stated to the

compilers that he recollected printing 15 or 20 copies each of this and other fragments of *Work in Progress* for Donald Friede. Friede disclaims any knowledge of the pamphlets either as publisher or as a recipient of copies.

32. ANNA LIVIA PLURABELLE 1928

First edition:

ANNA LIVIA PLURABELLE | BY JAMES JOYCE | WITH A PREFACE | BY PADRAIC COLUM | [publisher's emblem] | NEW YORK: CROSBY GAIGE: 1928

COLLATION: [4], xx, 64 pp. $[1–11]^4$. 17.5 x 11.3 cm., top edge gilt, other edges untrimmed. Printed on cream-white wove paper watermarked: NAVARRE Cream-white end papers. The first signature was specially folded to bring the limitation statement (for the author's signature) on the final page of the signature.

PAGINATION: pp.[1–4], blank; p.[i], fly title; p.[ii], blank; p.[iii], title page; p.[iv], copyright notice, statement of limitation and printing: *Copyright : 1928 : Crosby Gaige* | *No.* [number written in ink] | *Eight hundred copies printed* | *Distributed in America by Random House* | *Each copy signed by the author* | *Typography by Frederic Warde* | [signature in ink *James Joyce*] | *Printed in the United States of America* ; p.[v], divisional half-title: *Preface* ; p.[vi], blank; pp. vii–[xix], text of *Preface by Padraic Colum* ; p.[xx], blank; p.[1], half-title; p.[2], blank; pp. 3–[61], text; pp.[62–4], blank.

BINDING: Brown cloth. Front cover blind stamped with border of three rules, the inner rule dentelle; in center, gilt-stamped, inverted triangle of three rules, the inner rule dentelle. Spine, gilt stamped: [two rules] | [ornamental rule] | ANNA | LIVIA | PLURA- | BELLE | [ornament] | JOYCE | [ornamental rule] | [rule] | [ornamental rule] | [ornament] | [ornamental rule] | [rule] | [ornamental rule] | GAIGE | [ornamental rule] | [two rules] Back cover same as front cover without gilt-stamped triangle. Brown and yellow striped headband and tailband.

PUBLICATION DATE AND PRICE: October 20, 1928. $15.

NUMBER OF COPIES: 850.

NOTES: This book was printed for Crosby Gaige by the Princeton University Press. FW 196–216.

A special issue of *Anna Livia Plurabelle* in this edition was printed on pale green-tinted paper, watermarked: *Alexandra Japan Made in U. S. A.* Pale green end papers. Binding same as above but in black cloth instead of brown. According to records of the Princeton University Press now in the Slocum Library, 50 copies of this special issue were printed. Copies of this special issue were neither numbered nor signed by Joyce. Of these 50 copies probably 6 were offered for sale by the publisher. These were numbered 1 to 6, with the following notice on p.[iv] in the handwriting of Crosby Gaige: *This is one of 6 copies on green paper. Crosby Gaige* . Apparently issued in a slip case of quarter green leather made by the Scroll Book Club (William G. Lummis). The Slocum Library copy is No. 4.

The remaining 44 copies were presumably given away by Crosby Gaige, with the exception of a few which were remaindered to the Chaucer Head Book Shop, New York, in 1938 by Random House.

33. ANNA LIVIA PLURABELLE 1930

First English edition:

ANNA LIVIA | PLURABELLE | FRAGMENT OF | *WORK IN PROGRESS* | BY | JAMES JOYCE | LONDON | FABER & FABER | 24 RUSSELL SQUARE

COLLATION: 32 pp. A single unsigned quire of 16 leaves. 18.9 x 12.8 cm., top edge trimmed, other edges untrimmed. Printed on cream-white laid paper; cream-white end papers watermarked: [crown] | Abbey Mills | Greenfield End papers sewn with the quire.

PAGINATION: p.[1], series note stating this is *Criterion Miscellany No. 15* and fly title; p.[2], blank; p.[3], title page; p.[4], printing history and printer: *This edition* | *first published in MCXXX* [*sic*] | *by Faber and Faber Limited* | *24 Russell Square London W.C.1* | *Printed in Great Britain* | *by Trend and Company Plymouth* | *All rights reserved* ; pp. 5–32, text.

BINDING: Brown cloth. Front cover, gilt stamped: CRITERION MISCELLANY—*No.* 15 | [decorative rule] | ANNA LIVIA | PLURABELLE | [star] | JAMES JOYCE Issued in transparent tissue protective wrapper.

PUBLICATION DATE AND PRICE: June 12, 1930. 2*s.*

NUMBER OF COPIES: In a letter to the compilers, June 11, 1948,

Faber & Faber stated that 10,166 copies of *Anna Livia Plurabelle* were sold in cloth and paper bindings. They have no record of the sales of separate printings. The book is out of print.

NOTES: Inserted in the volume are three single sheets advertising "Mr. Joyce's own reading of the last four pages of *Anna Livia Plurabelle*" (The Orthological Institute), "James Joyce's *Ulysses*" by Stuart Gilbert (Faber & Faber), and *The Criterion.*

This edition was also issued in cinnamon-colored covers, printed in red. Publication price, 1*s*. The issue in covers was reprinted in June 1930 (twice) and in October 1932.

34. WORK IN PROGRESS PART 13 [1928]

[ornamental border] | [light rule] | [heavy rule] | JAMES JOYCE | [rule] | Work in Progress | Part 13 | [heavy rule] | [light rule] | [ornamental border]
[Note: The foregoing appears on the front cover, which is used as the title page.]

COLLATION: 40 pp. A single unsigned quire of 10 folio leaves, stapled. 19.6 x 13.9 cm., all edges trimmed. Printed on cream-white wove paper.

PAGINATION: pp. 1–38, text, with heading on p. 1: *Continuation of a Work | in Progress* [1] | *by James Joyce* . Footnote (1) refers to previous publication of this and other portions in *transition;* pp. [39–40], blank.

BINDING: Buff covers, stapled. Front cover, serving as title page, printed as above.

PUBLICATION DATE AND PRICE: August 15, 1928. Printed for copyright purposes and not for sale.

NUMBER OF COPIES: 5.

NOTES: No notice of copyright appears in this work.

The text of *Part 13*, originally printed in *transition*, Paris, 13 (Summer 1928), appears as FW 429–73.

Five copies of this publication were ordered by Joyce's New York legal representatives on October 4, 1928. Two copies were received at the Copyright Office on November 9, 1928, and copyright was issued as of August 15, 1928.

Only one copy of *Work in Progress Part 13* has been located. It is in the Library of Congress.

For a further account of the circumstances of publication of this work see the note under *Work in Progress Part 11 and 12* (A 31).

35. WORK IN PROGRESS PART 15 [1929]

[ornamental border] | [light rule] | [heavy rule] | JAMES JOYCE | [rule] | Work in Progress | Part 15 | [heavy rule] | [light rule] | [ornamental border]
[Note: The foregoing appears on the front cover, which is used as the title page.]

COLLATION: 56 pp. A single unsigned quire of 14 folio leaves, stapled. 19.4 x 14.3 cm., all edges trimmed. Printed on white laid paper.

PAGINATION: pp. 1–55, text, with heading on p. 1: *Continuation of a Work | in Progress*[1] *| by James Joyce* . Footnote (1) refers to previous publication of this and other portions in *transition;* p.[56], blank.

BINDING: Yellow covers, stapled. Front cover, serving as title page, printed as above.

PUBLICATION DATE AND PRICE: February 15, 1929. Printed for copyright purposes and not for sale.

NUMBER OF COPIES: 5.

NOTES: No notice of copyright appears in this work. The text of Part 15 originally printed in *transition*, Paris, 15 (Feb 1929), appears as FW 474–554.

Of the five copies of this publication ordered March 27, 1929, by Joyce's New York legal representatives, two copies were received at the Copyright Office on April 10, 1929. Copyright was issued as of February 15, 1929.

Two copies of *Work in Progress Part 15* have been located. They are in the Library of Congress and in the Slocum Library (formerly in the files of the New York law firm).

For a further account of the circumstances of publication of this work see the notes under *Work in Progress Part 11 and 12* (A 31).

36. TALES TOLD OF SHEM AND SHAUN 1929

First edition:

Tales Told of [in red] | Shem and Shaun [in red] | Three Fragments from | Work in Progress | by | JAMES JOYCE [in red] | THE BLACK SUN PRESS | RUE CARDINALE | PARIS | MCMXXIX

COLLATION: [14], XVI, 64 pp. $[1]^6$, $[2–11]^4$, plus a leaf tipped in after $[1]_6$. 21 x 16.5 cm., top edge trimmed, other edges untrimmed. Printed on cream-white laid paper watermarked: [monogram] | HOLLAND VAN GELDER ZONEN

PAGINATION: pp.[1–2], blank; p.[3], copyright: . . . *Copyrighted by James Joyce, 1929.* ; p.[4], blank (pp.[1–4] are inserted under the folding flaps of the outer front cover); pp.[5–6], blank; p.[7], fly title; p.[8], blank; p.[9], title page; p.[10], blank; p.[11], *Contents* ; pp.[12–13], blank; p.[14], portrait of the author by C. Brancusi, with tissue guard sheet; pp. I–XV, *Preface* by C. K. Ogden; p.[XVI], blank; pp. 1–55, text; p.[56], blank; p.[57], colophon: *This first edition | of Tales Told of Shem and Shaun by | James Joyce, with a preface by C. K. | Ogden and a portrait of the author by | Brancusi, printed in hand-set Caslon in | June 1929 for and under the direction | of Harry and Caresse Crosby at their | Black Sun Press (Maître-Imprimeur | Lescaret) Rue Cardinale, Paris, is limited | to 100 copies on Japanese Vellum signed | by the author, 500 copies on Holland | Van Gelder Zonen and 50 copies Hors | Commerce. | The entire edition is for sale at the | Bookshop of Harry F. Marks | 31 West 47 Street New York* | [number stamped in]; pp.[58–64], blank (pp.[61–4] are inserted under the folding flaps of the outer back cover).

BINDING: White paper covers with folding top and side flaps, covered with transparent protective tissue. Front cover printed exactly the same as the title page. Spine, reading from top to bottom, lettered vertically: FRAGMENTS JOYCE [in red] 1929 Back cover contains publisher's emblem in center. Issued in cardboard slip case covered with green suede paper edged with silver paper tape. Green ribbon pull.

PUBLICATION DATE AND PRICE: The New York Public Library copy has a tipped-in presentation slip from the Black Sun Press dated August 9, 1929. $20.

NUMBER OF COPIES: 650 (500 of this limitation).

NOTES: The copies printed on Japanese Vellum and signed by the author on the fly title, p.[7], have the number written out in pencil below the colophon on p.[57]. They were issued in a cardboard slip case covered with red suede paper edged with gilt paper tape and containing a red ribbon pull; the price was $30.

The copies *hors commerce* are on Van Gelder Zonen paper and are stamped H.C. below the colophon, p.[57].

A gilt slip case has also been noted. The slip cases of different colors were undoubtedly used interchangeably.

CONTENTS: *Portrait of the Author by C. Brancusi* ; *Preface by C. K. Ogden* ; *The Mookse and the Gripes* (FW 152–9) ; *The Muddest Thick That Was Ever Heard Dump* (FW 282–304) ; *The Ondt and the Gracehoper* (FW 414–19) .

37. TWO TALES OF SHEM AND SHAUN 1932

First English edition:

TWO TALES OF | SHEM AND SHAUN | FRAGMENTS FROM | *WORK IN PROGRESS* | BY | JAMES JOYCE | LONDON | FABER AND FABER | 24 RUSSELL SQUARE

COLLATION: 48 pp. [A]^4, B–F^4. 18.6 x 12.1 cm., all edges trimmed. Printed on cream-white wove paper; cream-white wove end papers.

PAGINATION: pp.[1–2], blank; p.[3], fly title; p.[4], blank; p.[5], title page; p.[6], printing history and printer: *First published in December MCMXXXII* | *by Faber and Faber Limited* | *24 Russell Square London W.C.1* | *Printed in Great Britain by* | *R. MacLehose and Company Limited* | *The University Press Glasgow* | *All rights reserved* ; p. 7, *Contents* ; p.[8], blank; pp. 9–45, text; pp.[46–8], blank.

BINDING: Pale green boards. Spine, stamped in blue, reading from top to bottom: TWO TALES OF SHEM AND SHAUN [star] JAMES JOYCE Issued in an orange dust wrapper, printed in blue.

PUBLICATION DATE AND PRICE: December 1, 1932. 2*s*. 6*d*.

NUMBER OF COPIES: In a letter, June 11, 1949, Faber & Faber stated that 3,849 copies were sold. The book is out of print.

NOTES: There is a copy of this book in the Slocum Library in dark green boards; priority not determined.

The Muddest Thick That Was Ever Heard Dump which appeared in *Tales Told of Shem and Shaun* (A 36) was omitted from this edition.

CONTENTS: *The Mookse and the Gripes* ; *The Ondt and the Gracehoper* .

38. WORK IN PROGRESS PART 18 1930

[ornamental border] | [light rule] | [heavy rule] | JAMES JOYCE | [rule] | Work in Progress | Part 18 | [heavy rule] | [light rule] | [ornamental border]

[Note: The foregoing appears on the front cover, which is used as the title page.]

COLLATION: 36 pp. A single unsigned quire of 9 folio leaves, stapled. 19.6 x 14.6 cm., all edges trimmed. Printed on white laid paper.

PAGINATION: Inner front cover bears copyright notice: *Copyright, 1930, by | James Joyce* ; pp. 1–34, text, with heading on p. 1: *Continuation of a Work | in Progress*[1] | *by James Joyce* . Footnote (1) refers to previous publication of this and other portions in *transition;* pp. [35–6], blank.

BINDING: Light tan covers, printed in blue, stapled. Front cover, serving as title page, printed as above. Copyright notice on inner front cover.

PUBLICATION DATE AND PRICE: January 7, 1930. Printed for copyright purposes and not for sale.

NUMBER OF COPIES: 5.

NOTES: The text of Part 18, originally printed in *transition*, Paris, 18 (Nov 1929), appears as FW 555–90.

Five copies of this publication were ordered by Joyce's New York legal representatives on December 17, 1929. Their Washington representative wrote the New York law firm on January 9, 1930, that this and previous publications of *Work in Progress* omitted the name of the printer, date, and name of copyright holder, all of which are required by law to make copyright valid, but that he had submitted two copies anyway. A lively exchange of letters between Washington and New York followed, and three remaining copies of *Part 18* were returned to Maisel and Company to have inserted on the reverse of the front cover the following copyright notice: *Copyright, 1930, by James Joyce.* Two of these three copies were then sent to Washington and were received at the Copyright Office on January 17, 1930. Copyright was issued as of January 7, 1930.

Only one copy of *Part 18* has been located. It is in the Slocum Library and was formerly in the files of the law firm. At the request of the compilers the Copyright Office consulted its files and said that the other four copies (two with copyright notice and two without) had all been returned to the claimant in accordance with policy current at the time of publication. The Washington representative of Joyce's New York attorney disclaimed any knowledge of these copies and said he had destroyed his old files. If the printer followed instructions and printed only five copies, the above is the only existing copy of *Part 18*.

For a further account of the circumstances of publication of this work see the notes under *Work in Progress Part 11 and 12* (A 31).

39. JAMES CLARENCE MANGAN 1930

First edition:

James Clarence Mangan | [From *St. Stephen's*, DUBLIN, May, 1902.] | BY | *James A. Joyce* | [publisher's emblem] | [rule] | ULYSSES BOOKSHOP | 187, High Holborn, London, W. C. 2 [2 changed in ink to 1] | [rule]

COLLATION: [xvi], 24 pp. [1–2]^4, [3]^8, [4]^4. 14.4 x 11.3 cm., all edges untrimmed. Printed on cream-white wove paper.

PAGINATION: pp. [i–ii], blank and glued to front cover; pp. [iii–xi], blank; p. [xii], limitation notice: *40 copies of this book* | *have been printed for* | *Private circulation.* | *No.* [number printed in] | *No copy for sale.* ; p. [xiii], title page; p. [xiv], blank; p. [xv], half-title; p. [xvi], blank; pp. 1–[16], text; pp. [17–22], blank; pp. [23–4], blank and glued to back cover.

BINDING: Quarter black cloth with purple boards. Front cover has a white label, printed in black: JAMES CLARENCE MANGAN | JOYCE

PUBLICATION DATE AND PRICE: March 7, 1930. Not for sale.

NUMBER OF COPIES: 40; number of review and out-of-series copies not ascertained.

NOTES: At the end of the text at the bottom of p.[16] is the following note: *7 : 3 : 30* | *Printed for The Ulysses Bookshop by H. D. C. Pepler.* [St. Dominic's Press]. The proprietor of the Ulysses Bookshop was Jacob Schwartz.

Shortly after their publication the publisher of *James Clarence Mangan* and *Ibsen's New Drama* wrote Joyce that 22 copies were sent to libraries, 10 to friends, and one each to Joyce, Stuart Gilbert, and Harriet Shaw Weaver, leaving him with about 5 sets. He assured Joyce that none were or ever would be offered for sale.

For the original publication of this article see C 2.

40. IBSEN'S NEW DRAMA 1930

First edition:

Ibsen's New Drama | [From *The Fortnightly Review* LONDON April 1900] . | BY | *James A. Joyce* | [publisher's emblem] | [rule] | ULYSSES BOOKSHOP | 187, High Holborn, London, W. C. 2 [2 changed in ink to 1] | [rule]

COLLATION: [xvi], 48 pp. [1–2]^{4}, [3–4]^{8}, [5–6]^{4}. 14.3 x 11.3 cm., all edges untrimmed. Printed on cream-white wove paper.

PAGINATION: pp.[i–ii], blank and glued to front cover; pp.[iii–xi], blank; p.[xii], limitation notice: *40 copies of this book* | *have been printed for* | *Private circulation.* | *No.* [number printed in] | *No copy for sale.* ; p.[xiii], title page; p.[xiv], blank; p.[xv], half-title; p.[xvi], blank; pp. 1–[37], text; pp.[38–46], blank; pp.[47–8], blank and glued to back cover.

BINDING: Quarter black cloth with purple boards. Front cover has a white label, printed in black: IBSEN'S NEW DRAMA | JOYCE

PUBLICATION DATE AND PRICE: March 11, 1930. Not for sale.

NUMBER OF COPIES: 40; number of review and out-of-series copies not ascertained.

NOTES: At the end of the text at the bottom of p.[37] is the following note: *Printed for The Ulysses Bookshop by H. D. C. Pepler* [St. Dominic's Press] | *11 : 3 : 30*

There is a copy of this book in the Slocum Library in which the 2 on the title page has not been changed to 1 in ink. In the limitation notice on p.[xii] this copy has [Press Copy] after the third line and omits the words *No copy for sale* .

For additional information on this book see the notes to *James Clarence Mangan* (A 39).

For the original publication of this article see C 1.

41. HAVETH CHILDERS EVERYWHERE 1930

First edition:

HAVETH CHILDERS [in green] | EVERYWHERE [in green] | *FRAGMENT FROM* | WORK IN PROGRESS | by | JAMES JOYCE | HENRY BABOU AND JACK KAHANE [in green] | *PARIS* | THE FOUNTAIN PRESS.—NEW YORK | 1930

COLLATION: 3–74 pp. [1–9]^4, plus two folio end papers sewn in and one leaf of each attached to front and back cover. 28.2 x 19 cm., untrimmed and unopened. Printed on white handmade pure linen Vidalon Royal paper, watermarked: VIDALON HAUT

PAGINATION: folio end paper; p.[3], fly title; p.[4], limitation notice: *This volume constituting the only | complete original edition of a | fragment of Work in Progress, | composed by hand in freshly cast | Elzévir Corps 16, comprises: 100 | copies on imperial hand-made irides- | cent Japan, signed by the writer | N°s 1 to 100; 500 copies on hand- | made pure linen Vidalon Royal | (specially manufactured for this | edition) N°s 101 to 600; half of | each category being for the United | States of America. There have also | been printed: 10 copies called | writer's copies on imperial hand- | made iridescent Japan, N^{os}* I *to* X; | *75 copies called writer's co- | pies on pure linen hand-made | Vidalon Royal, N^{os}* XI *to* LXXXV. | *Copy N^o* [number stamped in]; p.[5], title page; p.[6], copyright notice: . . . *Copyright by Henry Babou and Jack Kahane, France 1930.* ; pp. 7–[73], text; p.[74], printer: *Printed and made in France by Ducros et Colas | Master-printers, Paris 1930* ; folio end paper.

BINDING: White paper covers, printed in black and green. Front cover: HAVETH CHILDERS [in green] | EVERYWHERE [in green] | BY | JAMES JOYCE Spine, reading from bottom to top: JAMES JOYCE [rule] HAVETH CHILDERS EVERYWHERE Covered by a transparent tissue protective wrapper. Issued in green slip case with gilt edges and facings.

PUBLICATION DATE AND PRICE: June 1930. $20.

NUMBER OF COPIES: 685 (500 of this issue).

NOTES: The 100 copies printed on imperial handmade iridescent Japan paper were signed by Joyce in pencil under the limitation notice on p.[4]. Some copies were enclosed in a three-panel wrapper of stiff cardboard covered with gilt paper, within the slip case described above. Price, $40. FW 532–54.

There is an account of the publication of this book in Jack Kahane, *Memoirs of a Booklegger*, London, Michael Joseph, [1939].

42. HAVETH CHILDERS EVERYWHERE 1931

First English edition:

HAVETH CHILDERS | EVERYWHERE | FRAGMENT OF | *WORK IN PROGRESS* | BY | JAMES JOYCE | LONDON | FABER & FABER | 24 RUSSELL SQUARE

COLLATION: 36 pp. A single unsigned quire of 18 leaves. 18.8 x 12.7 cm., top edge trimmed, other edges untrimmed. Printed on cream-white laid paper; cream-white end papers.

PAGINATION: p.[1], series note stating this is *Criterion Miscellany No. 26* and fly title; p.[2], blank; p.[3], title page; p.[4], printing history and printer: *This edition* | *first published in* MCMXXXI | *by Faber and Faber Limited* | *24 Russell Square London W.C.1* | *Printed in Great Britain* | *by Trend and Company Plymouth* | *All rights reserved* ; pp. 5–36, text.

BINDING: Canary yellow cloth. Front cover, gilt stamped: CRITERION MISCELLANY—*No. 26* | [decorative rule] | HAVETH CHILDERS | EVERYWHERE | [star] | JAMES JOYCE Issued in transparent tissue protective wrapper.

PUBLICATION DATE AND PRICE: May 8, 1931. 2*s.*

NUMBER OF COPIES: In a letter, June 11, 1948, Faber & Faber stated that 249 copies of the cloth issue and 5,341 copies of the paper-bound issues (in all printings) were sold. They have no records of the sales of separate printings. The book is out of print.

NOTES: This edition was also issued in yellow covers printed in red. Publication price, 1*s.* The issue in wrappers was reprinted in May 1933.

43. THE MIME OF MICK NICK AND THE MAGGIES 1934

First edition:

JAMES JOYCE [in red] | THE MIME OF MICK | NICK AND THE | MAGGIES | A FRAGMENT FROM [in red] | WORK IN PROGRESS [in red] | [publisher's emblem] | MCMXXXIV | THE SERVIRE PRESS [dot] THE HAGUE [in red]

COLLATION: [viii], 80 pp. [*]^4, [1]^8, 2–5^8. 24.3 x 16 cm., all edges untrimmed. Printed on white Old Antique Dutch laid paper.

PAGINATION: pp. [i–ii], blank; p. [iii], fly title; p. [iv], blank; p. [v], title page; p. [vi], notice of design and copyright: *The initial letter, tail-piece and cover | were specially designed by | Miss Lucia Joyce | All rights reserved | Copyright 1933 by N. V. Servire, The Hague (Holland)* ; pp. [vii–viii], blank; pp. 1–77, text; p. [78], blank; p. [79], colophon: *Colophon | Printed on the presses of G. J. Thieme at | Nymegen in | a) twenty-nine copies on Simili Japon of Van | Gelder Zonen, bound in parchment, num- | bered from I–XXIX (of which No. V– | XXIX are for sale), and signed by Mr. James | Joyce and Miss Lucia Joyce; | b) one thousand copies on Old Antique Dutch, | numbered from 1–1000. | The initial letter, the tailpiece and the cover | were specially designed for these editions by | Miss Lucia Joyce. | This copy is number* [number stamped in]; p. [80], blank.

BINDING: Stiff cream-white paper wrapper enclosed in cream-white paper covers glued to the spine and printed in blue. Front cover: THE MIME OF MICK, NICK | AND THE MAGGIES | [design by Lucia Joyce] | JAMES JOYCE Spine, reading from top to bottom: JAMES JOYCE [dot] THE MIME OF MICK, NICK AND THE MAGGIES Back cover: [publisher's emblem] | PRINTED IN | HOLLAND The front flap of the cover contains descriptive comment. Issued in transparent tissue or cellophane protective wrapper, enclosed in slip case.

PUBLICATION DATE AND PRICE: June 1934. 12*s.* 6*d.*, or $3.50.

NUMBER OF COPIES: 1,000, plus 29 special copies. In a letter, June 11, 1948, Faber & Faber stated that 300 copies were sold in the United Kingdom.

NOTES: The thousand copies described in the colophon were issued under four imprints: (1) the Servire Press, The Hague (as above); (2) Messageries Dawson, Paris; (3) Faber & Faber, London;

(4) Gotham Book Mart, New York. In numbers 2, 3, and 4 the additional imprint is added below that of the Servire Press on the title page and separated from it by a rule. FW 219–59.

The special copies were issued with the imprint of the Servire Press only. They were printed in Simili Japon of Van Gelder Zonen paper, watermarked: [monogram] | *Holland* . Top edge trimmed, fore edge untrimmed and unopened, bottom edge untrimmed. The colophon, p.[79], is numbered in ink and signed below by James Joyce and Lucia Joyce. These copies were bound in blue and gold linen over boards, gilt stamped. Front cover: [single rule rectangle] Spine, reading from top to bottom: JAMES JOYCE [dot] THE MIME OF MICK, NICK AND THE MAGGIES Issued in dust wrapper and protective tissue of the regular edition. Blue and cream patterned end papers. Issued in plain gray box.

Though a parchment binding is called for in the colophon, all copies of this special edition were apparently issued in blue and gold linen over boards.

Copies of the regular edition were issued in various slip cases. The slip case of Faber & Faber is silver, with a pink and silver label; the Gotham Book Mart slip case is of plain rough brown cardboard.

The book was printed with the Grotius character of S. H. de Roos.

44. COLLECTED POEMS 1936

First edition:

COLLECTED POEMS | OF | JAMES JOYCE | NEW YORK | THE BLACK SUN PRESS | 1936

COLLATION: [6], LXX pp. [1]^{6} [2–5]^{8}. 16.5 x 11.4 cm., untrimmed and unopened. Printed on white wove paper, watermarked: B F K FRANCE

PAGINATION: pp.[1–2], blank, glued to front cover; pp.[3–4], blank; p.[5], fly title; p.[6], blank; p.[I], title page; p.[II], copyright notice; p.[III], contents; p.[IV], blank; pp.[V]–LXV, text; p.[LXVI], colophon: *This first edition of The Collected Poems | consists of Chamber Music, reprinted by | courteous permission of The Viking Press, | Pomes Penyeach, hitherto unpublished in the | United States, and Ecce Puer, never before | included in any edition. The frontispiece | is from a crayon portrait of the author by | Augustus John reproduced by Ja-*

comet of | Paris. The book has been designed, set by | hand and printed under the direction of | Caresse Crosby in the City of New York | and is strictly limited to 800 numbered | copies of which copies 1 to 50 are printed on | Japan Vellum and signed by the author. | This copy is number | [number written in ink]; pp. [LXVII–LXVIII], blank; pp. [LXVIX–LXX], blank and glued to back cover. A sepia plate, not included in the pagination, is tipped in, with a tissue guard sheet, facing the title page: *James Joyce | Augustus John. | Paris | 1930*

BINDING: Cream-white boards, stamped in blue. Front cover: an all-over design of 23 floral ornaments within a border of floral decorations and rules. Spine, reading from top to bottom, lettered vertically: [two rules] | COLLECTED POEMS | [ornament] | JAMES JOYCE | [two rules] Cream-white headband and tailband; blue ribbon place mark. Issued in transparent tissue protective wrapper.

PUBLICATION DATE AND PRICE: December 1936. Earliest review noted: "Books," *New York Herald Tribune*, December 13, 1936. $5.

NUMBER OF COPIES: 800 (750 of this issue).

NOTES: The book is printed throughout in a blue italic type.

The special issue of 50 copies is printed on Japan Vellum, top edge gilt, other edges untrimmed. Joyce's signature appears on the Augustus John portrait facing the title page. The binding is the same as that of the regular edition but is stamped in gilt instead of blue. Issued in a plain gilt slip case. Price, $20.

45. COLLECTED POEMS 1937

COLLECTED POEMS | JAMES JOYCE | *New York* | *THE VIKING PRESS* | 1937 [Note: The foregoing is within a triple-rule box.]

COLLATION: 64 pp. [1–4]^{8}. 21.2 x 14.2 cm., all edges trimmed. Printed on cream-white wove paper; cream-white end papers.

PAGINATION: p. [1], fly title; p. [2], blank; p. [3], title page; p. [4], copyright notice and printer: . . . *Printed in the United States of America | by the Stratford Press | Distributed in Canada by the Macmillan Company of Canada, Ltd.* ; p. [5], contents; p. [6], blank; pp. [7]–63, text; p. [64], blank. Tipped in facing p. [2] and not included in the pagination is a reproduction of a crayon drawing of James Joyce by Augustus John, Paris, 1930.

BINDING: Rose cloth. Front cover, stamped in blind: [publisher's emblem] Spine, gilt stamped, reading from top to bottom: JAMES

JOYCE [dot] COLLECTED POEMS [dot] VIKING PRESS Issued in a rose-orange dust wrapper with black panels on spine, printed in white; the front cover has a reproduction of the Augustus John portrait of Joyce.

PUBLICATION DATE AND PRICE: September 1937. $2.

NUMBER OF COPIES: 1,000.

NOTES: This first trade edition of *Collected Poems* was reprinted in October 1937 (1,000 copies), October 1944 (1,000 copies), and March 1946 (2,500 copies).

Collected Poems is included in *The Portable James Joyce* (A 55).

There has been no separate English edition of *Collected Poems*, but they are included in *The Essential James Joyce* (A 56).

46. STORIELLA AS SHE IS SYUNG 1937

First edition:

STORIELLA | AS SHE IS | SYUNG

COLLATION: [56]pp. [1–7]^4 (front and back lining papers are part of first and last signatures). 32.3 x 26 cm., top edge gilt, other edges untrimmed. Printed on Arnold handmade paper, watermarked: UN-BLEACHED ARNOLD

PAGINATION: pp.[1–2], blank and glued to front cover; pp.[3–12], blank; p.[13], title page; p.[14], blank; p.[15], subtitle: A SECTION | OF "WORK IN | PROGRESS" BY | JAMES JOYCE ; p.[16], blank; pp.[17–43], text; p.[44], blank; p.[45], statement on text and decoration: *This book | comprises the | opening and | closing pages | of part II: sec = | tion II: of "Work | in Progress." The | illuminated | capital letter | at the beginning | is the work of | Lucia Joyce | the author's | daughter* ; p.[46], blank; p.[47], colophon: *Of this book One Hundred and Seventy- | five copies have been set in 18-pt. | Centaur type and printed on Arnold | hand-made paper. All copies have been | numbered from 1 to 175. One extra | copy lettered "A" has been printed on a | white Japanese mulberry paper and is | reserved for the printer. Copies Nos. 1 | to 25 have been signed by the Author. | This copy is number* [number written in ink] | *Completed at the Corvinus Press during | October, 1937. Laus Deo.* ; pp.[48–54], blank; pp.[55–6], blank and glued to back cover.

BINDING: Flexible orange vellum, gilt stamped. Front cover: STO-

RIELLA | AS SHE IS | SYUNG Spine, reading from bottom to top: STORIELLA AS SHE IS SYUNG. A SECTION OF WORK IN PROGRESS BY JAMES JOYCE. Back cover: [publisher's emblem] White headband. Issued in a plain gray-green slip case.

PUBLICATION DATE AND PRICE: October 1937. £2 2s.; £3 3s. (signed copies).

NUMBER OF COPIES: 176 (150 of this issue).

NOTES: This edition was printed and published by Lord Carlow of the Corvinus Press, London. FW 260–75, 304–8.

Throughout the book the marginal commentary is printed in red at the right of the page, in black at the left.

The special issue of 25 copies is the same as the above, except for Joyce's signature in the colophon and a variation in the binding. The binding is of orange vellum over stiff boards, stamped the same as the regular issue but with a thonged spine. The first and last signatures are not sewn; in the first signature leaves 1 and 2 have been glued to the front cover, all but the margin of leaf 1 having first been cut away; similarly, leaves 3 and 4 have been glued to the back cover, all but the margin of leaf 4 having first been cut away. The special issue was also issued in a plain gray-green slip case.

The printer's copy "A" is still in the possession of his heirs.

47. FINNEGANS WAKE 1939

First English edition (regular):

FINNEGANS | WAKE | by | James Joyce | London | Faber and Faber Limited

COLLATION: [viii], 628 pp. [*]^4, [A]^8, B–2Q^8, plus a folio leaf, $2Q_2$ inserted after 2Q. 24.2 x 15.5 cm., top edge stained orange-yellow, other edges untrimmed. Printed on cream-white wove paper; cream-white end papers.

PAGINATION: pp. [i–iv], blank; p. [v], fly title; p. [vi], list of books *by the same writer* ; p. [vii], title page; p. [viii], printing history and printer: *First published in Mcmxxxix | by Faber and Faber Limited | 24 Russell Square London W.C.1 | Printed in Great Britain by | R. MacLehose and Company Limited | The University Press Glasgow | All rights reserved* ; p. [1], divisional numeral: I ; p. [2], blank; pp. [3]–216, text of Part I; p. [217], divisional numeral: II ; p. [218], blank; pp. 219–399, text of Part II; p.[400], blank; p.[401], divisional numeral: III ; p.[402], blank; pp. 403–590, text of Part III; p.[591], divisional numeral: IV ; p.[592], blank; pp.593–628, text of Part IV.

BINDING: Rough red cloth. Spine, gilt stamped on two panels stamped in blind. Top panel: [three rules] | FINNEGANS | WAKE | [three rules] | JAMES JOYCE | [three rules] Bottom panel: [three rules] | FABER & FABER | [three rules] Issued in a red and yellow dust wrapper.

PUBLICATION DATE AND PRICE: May 4, 1939. 25*s.*

NUMBER OF COPIES: A letter from Faber & Faber, June 11, 1948, states: "The ordinary edition consisted of 3400 copies of which 2255 were sold to the public, 950 in the form of sheets being destroyed. The balance were gratis, etc."

NOTES: Of their current (1948) title in stock, Faber & Faber write: "The no. printed to date is 2264 in two printings, the first being of 1014 and the second 1250. They have all been bound and sales to 31st May 1948 are 2163. This edition was published 24th Sept. 1946. Price 30s." *Finnegans Wake* was again reprinted later in 1948. The reprints are of a slightly smaller format than the original regular edition. In the 1946 and later printings "Corrections of Misprints" is added, pp. 1–28, at the end of the volume. Some of the misprints have been corrected in the text and omitted from the "Corrections of Misprints."

48. FINNEGANS WAKE 1939

First American edition (regular):

FINNEGANS | WAKE | *James Joyce* | New York: The Viking Press | 1939

COLLATION: [vi], 630 pp. The signatures of the first regular English edition were retained as follows: [***], A–R^8, [S]^8, T–2Q^8, plus 2Q$_2$. The book is, however, sewn in 16's, except the last quire which is sewn in 14. 24.1 x 15.3 cm., top edge stained green, other edges trimmed. Printed on Warren's Eggshell, white, Substance 50. White end papers.

PAGINATION: pp.[i–ii], blank; p.[iii], fly title; p.[iv], list of books *by the same writer* ; p.[v], title page; p.[vi], copyright notice and printer: *First published May 1939 | Finnegans Wake | Copyright 1939 by James Joyce | Printed in the United States of America | by the*

Reehl Litho Company | *Distributed in Canada* | *by the Macmillan Company of Canada, Limited* ; p.[1], divisional numeral: I ; p.[2], blank; pp.[3]–216, text of Part I; p.[217], divisional numeral: II ; p.[218], blank; pp. 219–399, text of Part II; p.[400], blank; p.[401], divisional numeral: III ; p.[402], blank; pp. 403–590, text of Part III; p.[591], divisional numeral: IV ; p.[592], blank; pp. 593–628, text of Part IV; pp.[629–30], blank.

BINDING: Black buckram, square backed, gilt stamped. Front cover: FINNEGANS WAKE | *James Joyce* Spine: FINNE- | GANS | WAKE | *James Joyce* | Viking Press Red and gold headband and tailband. Issued in a gray, slate-green, and red dust wrapper.

PUBLICATION DATE AND PRICE: May 4, 1939. $5.

NUMBER OF COPIES: 6,000.

NOTES: A letter from the Viking Press, September 9, 1947, states: "The trade edition, of which there were four printings, was printed in the United States by offset from reproduction proofs supplied by the English publisher, and the composition cost was shared by Faber & Faber and the Viking Press."

Finnegans Wake was reprinted September 1943 (1,000 copies), October 1944 (2,000), October 1945 (3,000), and March 1947 (5,700). The "Corrections of Misprints" were bound in with the March 1947 printing.

49. FINNEGANS WAKE 1939

First edition (*limited*):

FINNEGANS | WAKE | by | James Joyce | 1939 | London: Faber & Faber Limited | New York: The Viking Press

COLLATION: [viii], 628 pp. [*]^4, [A]^8, B–2Q^8, plus a folio leaf, 2Q$_2$ inserted after 2Q. 25.4 x 16.5 cm., top edge gilt, other edges untrimmed. Printed on cream-white wove paper; cream-white end papers.

PAGINATION: pp.[i–ii], blank; p.[iii], statement of limitation: *This signed edition is limited to* | *four hundred and twenty-five numbered copies* | *of which one hundred and twenty-five copies* | *are for sale in Great Britain* | *and three hundred copies* | *in the United States of America* | *This copy is number* [number written in ink] | [signature of James Joyce]; p.[iv], blank; p.[v], fly title; p.[vi], blank; p.[vii], title page; p.[viii], printer: *Printed in Great Britain | by R. MacLehose & Company Limited | The University Press Glasgow* ; p.[1], divisional numeral: I ; p.[2], blank; pp.[3]–216, text of Part I; p. [217], divisional numeral: II ; p.[218], blank; pp. 219–399, text of Part II; p.[400], blank; p.[401], divisional numeral: III ; p.[402], blank; pp. 403–590, text of Part III; p.[591], divisional numeral: IV ; p.[592], blank; pp. 593–628, text of Part IV.

BINDING: Smooth brick red buckram. Spine, gilt stamped on two panels stamped in blind. Top panel: [three rules] | FINNEGANS | WAKE | [three rules] | JAMES JOYCE | [three rules] Bottom panel: [three rules] | MCMXXXIX | [three rules] Yellow headband. Issued in a slip case covered with yellow cloth.

PUBLICATION DATE AND PRICE: May 4, 1939. £5 5s. $25.

NUMBER OF COPIES: 425. A letter from the Viking Press, September 9, 1947, states: "We also brought out and sold a limited edition of 310 copies the sheets of which were imported from the English publisher Faber & Faber. Our limited edition is identical with that of the British publisher and bears both imprints. The covers for the limited edition were made in England but the actual binding was done in the United States." 310 copies were sent to the United States instead of the 300 noted in the statement of limitation.

50. PASTIMES 1941

First edition:

***Pastimes** of | JAMES JOYCE*

COLLATION: [12] pp. [1][6]. A single unsigned quire of 3 folio leaves stapled twice. 27.8 x 21.5 cm., all edges trimmed. Printed on cream-white wove paper.

PAGINATION: p.[1], blank; p.[2], reproduction of a pencil portrait of Joyce by Jo Davidson; p.[3], title page; p.[4], copyright notice: *Copyright 1941 | by the Joyce Memorial Fund Committee | Printed in U. S. A.* ; p.[5], text, signed by *Maria McDonald Jolas New York April 1941* ; pp.[6–7], facsimile reproduction of a holograph "Come-all-ye," signed *J.J. Thanksgiving Day 1937* ; p.[8], text, signed by *Padraic Colum* ; p.[9], facsimile reproduction of Thomas Moore's poem "At the Mid Hour of Night" in Joyce's hand with his scansion marks; p.[10], blank; p.[11], colophon: *This first appearance of Pastimes is limited to 100 numbered copies on | Montgomery offset paper bound in Hurlbut's Shadowmould, signed | by Maria Jolas, Padraic Colum and Jo Davidson for sale at five | dollars, 700 copies unsigned in wrappers at one dollar. | Both editions issued by the Joyce Memorial Fund | Committee, distributed by Gotham Book | Mart, 51 West 47th Street, New York. | The entire proceeds to be forwarded | to the family of James Joyce. | No.* [number stamped in]; p.[12], blank.

BINDING: Blue-gray paper covers, stapled. Front cover, printed in black: *James Joyce* [facsimile signature] at bottom right.

PUBLICATION DATE AND PRICE: May 1941. $1. $5 (signed).

NUMBER OF COPIES: 800 (700 of this issue).

NOTES: The 100 signed copies were bound in blue-gray boards, with the facsimile signature of Joyce on the front cover, and issued in a transparent tissue protective wrapper. The leaf measures 30.1 x 22.6 cm.; there are blue-gray end papers and the quire is stitched through the center fold. The numbering on p.[11] is in ink and is followed by the signatures of Maria Jolas, Padraic Colum, and Jo Davidson. Price, $5.

Copies sold at the time of publication do not bear Jo Davidson's signature; he was in South America at that time.

51. STEPHEN HERO 1944

First edition:

STEPHEN HERO | *Part of the first draft of* | *'A Portrait of the Artist as a Young Man'* | by | JAMES JOYCE | [publisher's emblem] | *Edited with an Introduction by* | THEODORE SPENCER | JONATHAN CAPE | THIRTY BEDFORD SQUARE | LONDON

COLLATION: 210 pp. [A]^8, B–N^8, plus leaf N* tipped in after N_1. 19.2 x 12.5 cm., top and fore edges trimmed, bottom edge untrimmed. Printed on cream-white wove paper; cream-white end papers.

PAGINATION: p.[1], fly title; p.[2], list of four books *By the same author* ; p.[3], title page; p.[4], publishing statement and printer: *First published 1944 | Jonathan Cape Ltd. 30 Bedford Square, London | and 91 Wellington Street West, Toronto* | [Book production war economy standard device and statement] | *Printed in Great Britain in the City of Oxford | at the Alden Press | Paper made by John*

Dickinson & Co. Ltd. | *Bound by A. W. Bain & Co. Ltd.* ; pp. 5–15, *Introduction* ; p. 16, *Editorial Note* ; pp.17–210, text.

BINDING: Black cloth, gilt stamped. Spine, reading from bottom to top: STEPHEN HERO [device] JAMES JOYCE Issued in a cream-white pictorial dust wrapper, printed in red; the front cover illustration is signed *N. I. Cannon.*

PUBLICATION DATE AND PRICE: July 24, 1944. 9*s.* 6*d.*

NUMBER OF COPIES: 2,000.

NOTES: An edition of *Stephen Hero* printed from the same plates as the first edition was issued by Star Editions, London, "for sale on the Continent of Europe only," in 1948. The Star edition was slightly smaller in format than the Jonathan Cape edition, bound in blue and white paper covers printed in orange, blue, and white, and sold for 5*s.*, or its Continental equivalent. Page [4] differed from the first edition in that it carried the imprint of Star Editions, date of first publication, and printer (same as in the first edition) only.

A description of the manuscript of *Stephen Hero* will be found in the manuscript section of this bibliography (E 3*b.i–ii*).

52. STEPHEN HERO 1944

First American edition:

STEPHEN [in pale green] | HERO [in pale green] | A PART OF THE FIRST DRAFT OF | *A Portrait of the Artist as a Young Man* | By JAMES JOYCE | [silhouette map of Ireland in pale green] | Edited from the manuscript in the Harvard College Library | by THEODORE SPENCER | A NEW DIRECTIONS BOOK

COLLATION: 236 pp. $[1\text{–}6]^{16}$, $[7]^{14}$, $[8]^{8}$. 23.3 x 15.5 cm., all edges trimmed. Printed on cream-white laid paper, watermarked: FLEMISH BOOK | MADE IN U.S.A. Cream-white wove end papers.

PAGINATION: p.[1], fly title; p.[2], blank; p.[3], title page; p.[4], copyright and publishing statement: *Copyright 1944 by New Directions* | *Manufactured in the United States of America* | *by the Vail-Ballou Press, Inc., Binghamton, N.Y.* | *New Directions Books are published by James Laughlin* | *New York Office—67 West 44, NYC—18* ; p.[5], divisional half-title: *Introduction & Editorial Note* | *Theodore Spencer* ; p.[6], blank; pp.7–18, *Introduction* ; pp.18–19, *Editorial Note* ; p.[20], blank; p.[21], divisional half-title: *The Manu-*

script of Stephen Hero ; p.[22], blank; pp.23–234, text; pp.[235–6], blank. The following plates have been tipped in and are not included in the pagination: facing title page, *From the portrait drawing of James Joyce* [by Augustus John] *in the Collection of Mrs. Murray Crane* ; facing p. 100, *University College Literary and Historical Society, Programme of Session 1899–1900.* [listing] *"Drama and Life." Paper. Mr. Joyce.* [for] *Sat. Jan. 20. Reproduced from the copy of the original in the Collection of John Jermain Slocum* ; facing p. 124, *George Clancy, J. F. Byrne ("Cranly") and James Joyce during University College Days* ; facing p. 194, *A Photostat of Page 827 of the Manuscript*

BINDING: Quarter black cloth, with sides of pale green boards. Spine, gilt stamped, reading from top to bottom, lettered vertically: STEPHEN HERO Issued in black, white, and pale green dust wrapper, the front cover containing a facsimile of a page of Joyce's manuscript and a silhouette map of Ireland, both in pale green, and the title and author printed in white.

PUBLICATION DATE AND PRICE: November 16, 1944. $3.50.

NUMBER OF COPIES: 3,000.

NOTES: The following note by Theodore Spencer appears on p. 18:

> This edition of *Stephen Hero* has recently appeared in England [Jonathan Cape]. As a result of war conditions it was not thought expedient to send proofs across the Atlantic, hence a few minor inaccuracies and one or two editorial divergencies from this American edition occur in the English text. I mention the fact in case some student of Joyce should compare the two; circumstances have made it possible for the American edition to be a more considered and accurate reproduction of the details of the Manuscript.

A second edition of *Stephen Hero* was issued by New Directions in 1945, bound in black cloth and in a smaller format.

53. CORRECTIONS OF MISPRINTS IN FINNEGANS WAKE 1945

First edition:

Corrections of Misprints in | FINNEGANS WAKE | BY JAMES JOYCE | As Prepared by the Author after | Publication of the First Edition | PUBLISHED 1945 BY | THE VIKING PRESS [dot] NEW YORK | for distribution to purchasers of | FINNEGANS WAKE

COLLATION: 16 pp. An unsigned quire of 4 folio leaves, stapled. 23.9 x 14.7 cm., all edges trimmed. Printed on cream-white wove paper.

PAGINATION: p.[1], title page (cover title); pp.2–16, text. At the bottom of p. 16: *Printed in U.S.A.*

PUBLICATION DATE AND PRICE: July 18, 1945. Distributed free to purchasers of *Finnegans Wake.*

NUMBER OF COPIES: 2,000.

NOTES: A letter from the Viking Press, October 3, 1947, states: "The errata sheet, of which I am enclosing a copy, was printed after the publication of both the regular and limited editions of *Finnegans Wake.* In announcing the errata sheet we offered to send it to such purchasers of the book as might request it. We do not have any copies of the English errata as prepared for Faber."

The English edition, printed for Faber & Faber, London, is exactly the same as the copy described above, except the imprint, which reads: PUBLISHED 1945 BY | FABER & FABER LTD [dot] LONDON | for distribution to purchasers of | FINNEGANS WAKE

The *Corrections of Misprints* were bound in the March 1947 American printing and in the 1946 and 1948 English printings (reset) of *Finnegans Wake.*

54. INTRODUCING JAMES JOYCE 1942

INTRODUCING | JAMES | JOYCE | a selection of Joyce's prose | by | T. S. ELIOT | with | an introductory note | FABER AND FABER LTD | 24 Russell Square | London

148 pp. 18.5 cm. Sesame books. 3*s.* 6*d.* Yellow cloth stamped in brown on spine. Yellow dust wrapper printed in brown. Published

October 23, 1942, in an edition of 5,000 copies; the verso of the title page gives the date (erroneously) as September. Reprinted. 16,414 copies were sold to May 31, 1948.

CONTENTS: "The Sisters" from *Dubliners*, *A Portrait of the Artist as a Young Man* (H 26–41, 234–46, 280–92), *Ulysses* (RH 25–37, 86–114, 287–92), *Finnegans Wake* (FW 152–9, 196–216, 619–28).

55. THE PORTABLE JAMES JOYCE 1947

THE PORTABLE | JAMES | JOYCE | WITH AN INTRODUCTION & NOTES | BY HARRY LEVIN | [publisher's emblem] | NEW YORK [dot] The Viking Press [dot] MCMXLVII

vi, 762 pp. 16.5 cm. Viking Portable Library. $2. Buff cloth stamped in brown and gilt. Brown and white dust wrapper, printed in brown and white. Published in December 1946 in an edition of 25,000 copies; the verso of the title page gives the date (erroneously) as January 1947. Reprinted.

CONTENTS: *Dubliners; A Portrait of the Artist as a Young Man; Exiles; Collected Poems; The Holy Office; Gas from a Burner; Ulysses:* "Nestor" (RH 30–7), "Hades" (RH 99–113), "The Wandering Rocks" (RH 238–40), "The Sirens" (RH 278–82), "Penelope" (RH 766–8); *Finnegans Wake:* "Here Comes Everybody" (FW 7–10, 15–18, 21–3), "Anna Livia Plurabelle" (FW 196–216), "Tales Told of Shem and Shaun" (FW 152–9, 414–19); bibliographical note. Each collection in this work contains a preface by the editor. The episodes from *Ulysses* are selections only.

This volume was reissued in 1949 by the Book Society, New York, as *The Indispensable James Joyce.*

56. THE ESSENTIAL JAMES JOYCE 1948

THE ESSENTIAL | JAMES JOYCE | With an Introduction and Notes by | HARRY LEVIN | [publisher's emblem] | JONATHAN CAPE | THIRTY BEDFORD SQUARE | LONDON

536 pp. 19.8 cm. *12s. 6d.* Brick red cloth, gilt stamped. Red and white dust wrapper, printed in black and red. Published in May 1948.

CONTENTS: Same as *The Portable James Joyce*, above, except for the omission of the bibliographical note.

B. *Books and Pamphlets with Contributions from James Joyce*

THE LISTINGS in this section are governed by the first appearance of the item in the country of publication.

* indicates first appearance in book form anywhere.

** indicates first appearance anywhere.

Because of its importance a full collation has been given for *Two Essays*, 1901.

1. "THE DAY OF THE RABBLEMENT"** 1901

Two Essays. | [wavy rule] | "A Forgotten Aspect of | the University Question" | BY | F. J. C. SKEFFINGTON | AND | "The Day of the Rabblement" | BY | JAMES A. JOYCE. | [double rule] | PRICE TWOPENCE. | [double rule] | Printed by | GERRARD BROS., | 37 STEPHEN'S GREEN, | DUBLIN.

[Note: The foregoing appears on the front cover which is used as the title page. It is enclosed in a double-rule border 18.7 x 11.2 cm., with ornamental corners and with decorative devices at top and bottom center.]

COLLATION: 8 pp. A single unsigned quire of 2 folio leaves, stapled. 21.3 x 13.5 cm., all edges trimmed. Printed on cream-white wove paper.

PAGINATION: p.[1], fly title; p.[2], preface: *Preface* | [decorative rule] | *These two Essays were commissioned by the Editor of* | *St. Stephen's for that paper, but were subsequently refused* | *insertion by the Censor. The writers are now publishing them* | *in their original form, and each writer is responsible only for* | *what appears under his own name.* | F. J. C. S. | J. A. J. ; pp.[3]–6, text of *A Forgotten Aspect of the University Question* ; pp.[7]–8, text of *The Day of the Rabblement*

BINDING: Pink covers with title as above; stapled.

PUBLICATION DATE AND PRICE: After October 15, 1901. 2*d.*

NOTES: P. 8 has the date *October 15th, 1901.* below the name *James A. Joyce* at the conclusion of the article.

A letter from P. S. O'Hegarty, Dublin, January 2, 1949, quotes Dr. Skeffington of Trinity College, Dublin, son of F. J. C. Sheehy-Skeffington: "Dr. Skeffington tells me there was nothing in his father's papers to give any clue to the number printed. He gave it as his opinion that it was at the most 200 and that it might be as low as 100, and I would be disposed to agree."

A Catalogue of Rare Books . . . issued by the Ulysses Bookshop, New York and London, 1933, item No. 144: "*Two Essays*. It was finally decided that 85 copies would be sufficient, for circulation and sale to the other members of the College."

A set of first proofs with corrections in the hand of the printer or of Sheehy-Skeffington is in the Slocum Library. Additional corrections as well as those in this set of first proofs were incorporated in the final texts.

Partly reprinted in Gorman, 1939, pp. 71–3; see also C 59 and 60.

2. THE VENTURE** [1904]

THE [in red] | VENTURE [in red] | AN ANNUAL | OF ART AND | LITERATURE | [publisher's device in red and black] | MCMV [in red] | JOHN BAILLIE | ONE PRINCES TERRACE | HEREFORD ROAD | LONDON. W.
[Note: The foregoing appears among torches and other decorative devices in red and black and is signed with the initials R L B]

x, 196 pp. 25.2 x 19 cm. 7*s*. 6*d*. Buff cloth with front cover illustration in black and orange.

Published in November 1904.

Contains "Two Songs I What counsel has the hooded moon . . . II Thou leanest to the shell of night, . . ." by James A. Joyce; p. 92. These poems which appear in *Chamber Music* as Nos. XII and XXVI constitute Joyce's first appearance in a book.

3. THE DUBLIN BOOK OF IRISH VERSE 1909

The | Dublin Book | Of Irish Verse | 1728–1909 | Edited by | John Cooke | Dublin | Hodges, Figgis & Co., Ltd. | London | Henry Frowde, Oxford University Press | 1909

viii, 804 pp. 18.5 x 12.1 cm. 7*s*. 6*d*. Dark green cloth, gilt stamped. Bottom of spine reads: DUBLIN | HODGES, | FIGGIS

Published in November 1909.

Contains "Strings in the Earth and Air," "Bid Adieu to Girlish Days," and "What Counsel Has the Hooded Moon," by James Joyce;

Two Essays.

"A Forgotten Aspect of the University Question"

BY

F. J. C. SKEFFINGTON

AND

"The Day of the Rabblement"

BY

JAMES A. JOYCE.

PRICE TWOPENCE.

Printed by
GERRARD BROS.,
37 STEPHEN'S GREEN,
DUBLIN.

TWO ESSAYS [1901] B1.

pp. 642–3. These poems appeared in *Chamber Music* as Nos. I, XI, and XII.

4. "I HEAR AN ARMY" 1914

DES IMAGISTES | AN ANTHOLOGY | [ornament] | NEW YORK | ALBERT AND CHARLES BONI | 96 FIFTH AVENUE | 1914

64 pp. 19 x 12.9 cm. $1. Blue cloth, gilt stamped.
Published March 2, 1914.

Contains "I Hear an Army," by James Joyce; p. 40. This poem appeared in *Chamber Music* as No. XXXVI. This anthology was a reprint of the *Glebe*, New York, 1.5 (Feb 1914), C 45. It was also published in England with the same sheets but with a different binding and end papers. On both the fly title and the title page of the English edition the following was inserted: LONDON: THE POETRY BOOKSHOP | 35 DEVONSHIRE STREET | THEOBALDS RD., W.C.

5. A CURIOUS HISTORY [1917]

From B. W. HUEBSCH, *Publisher*, NEW YORK | [rule] | 1. | We are indebted to *The Egoist* (London) for | this extraordinary account, by Ezra Pound, of the | difficulties that preceded the publication of "Dub- | liners" in Great Britain. James Joyce, the author | of that book and of "A Portrait of the Artist as | a Young Man," has established himself firmly in | the world of letters by these two books which have | been published in the United States by B. W. | Huebsch. | A Curious History

A broadside. 38 x 18.5 cm. Distributed free.
Published May 5, 1917, in an edition of 500 copies.

This promotional broadside is the first separate publication of *A Curious History*, reprinted from the *Egoist* 1.2 (Jan 15, 1914) 26–7. The text consists of a letter from Ezra Pound to the *Egoist* which includes two letters from James Joyce concerning the publication of *Dubliners*. Six lines of publisher's comments are added after the letter.

6. JAMES JOYCE: HIS FIRST FORTY YEARS 1924

JAMES JOYCE | HIS FIRST FORTY YEARS | by | HERBERT S. GORMAN | *Author of* "The Fool of Love," "The Barcarole | of James Smith," "The Procession | of Masks," *etc.* | [publisher's emblem] | NEW YORK B. W. HUEBSCH, INC. MCMXXIV

[viii], 240 pp. Illus. 18.9 x 12.7 cm. $2. Pebbled cloth, gilt and blind stamped. Dust wrapper.

Published March 17, 1924.

Contains a letter to the press, dated August 18, 1911 [*A Curious History*]; pp.34–6. Passages from *Ulysses;* pp.125, 129–31, 143, 144–6, 158, 161–3, 168, 172–3, 174–5, 189–91, 195–8, 200–2, 207, 210–12, facing 224. The passages through p. 175 represent material that had previously appeared in the *Little Review;* with the exception of the photograph of the first page of the manuscript of *Ulysses*, which appears facing p. 224 (reprinted from the Quinn Catalogue 1924), the quotations from p. 189 on appear in the United States for the first time.

Reissued in 1925 by the Viking Press and B. W. Huebsch.

Published in England by Geoffrey Bles in 1926 with American sheets but a new title page.

7. "FROM WORK IN PROGRESS"** 1925

CONTACT COLLECTION OF | CONTEMPORARY WRITERS | Djuna Barnes | Bryher | Mary Butts | Norman Douglas | Havelock Ellis | F. M. Ford | Wallace Gould | Ernest Hemingway | Marsden Hartley | H. D. | John Herrman [*sic*] | James Joyce | Mina Loy | Robert McAlmon | Ezra Pound | Dorothy Richardson | May Sinclair | Edith Sitwell | Gertrude Stein | W. C. Williams

viii, 340 pp. 19 x 14 cm. $3. Gray paper covers printed in black.

Colophon: PRINTED AT DIJON BY MAURICE DARANTIÈRE M.CM.XXV.

Published in an edition of 300 copies.

Contains "From Work in Progress," by James Joyce; pp. [133]–6 (FW 30–4, l. 29).

8. THE ROAD ROUND IRELAND 1926

THE ROAD ROUND | IRELAND———BY | PADRAIC COLUM | THE MACMILLAN COMPANY | PUBLISHERS : 1926 : NEW YORK

xviii, 492 pp. 19.7 x 13.8 cm. $4. Green cloth, gilt stamped. Dust wrapper.

Published September 29, 1926, in an edition of 5,037 copies.

Contains "What counsel has the hood [*sic*] moon," *Chamber Music*, XII; p. 311. Selections from *A Portrait of the Artist as a Young Man;* pp. 312–13, 322–3, 324–5. From *The Day of Rabblement* [*sic*]; pp. 314–15. From *The Holy Office;* p. 326. From *Ulysses;* pp. 328, 329–30.

9. "ALL OFF FOR A BUSTER" 1929

MERRY-GO-DOWN | A GALLERY OF GORGEOUS | DRUNKARDS THROUGH THE AGES | [vignette] | COLLECTED FOR THE USE INTEREST | ILLUMINATION AND DELECTATION OF | SERIOUS TOPERS | *by RAB NOOLAS* | AND DECORATED BY HAL COLLINS | [ornamental rule] | *THE MANDRAKE PRESS* 41 *MUSEUM STREET* | *LONDON*

xiv, 232 pp. 28 x 19.2 cm. 42*s*. Brown cloth, gilt stamped. Dust wrapper.

Colophon: This edition is limited to 600 numbered copies.

Contains "All Off for a Buster," by James Joyce; pp. 224–8. These are the closing pages of Episode XIV of *Ulysses* (RH 417–21), here published in England for the first time.

"Rab Noolas" is a pseudonym of Philip Heseltine.

10. OUR EXAGMINATION . . .** 1929

OUR EXAGMINATION | ROUND HIS FACTIFICATION | FOR INCAMINATION | OF WORK IN PROGRESS | BY | SAMUEL BECKETT, MARCEL BRION, FRANK BUDGEN, | STUART GILBERT, EUGENE JOLAS, VICTOR LLONA, | ROBERT MCALMON, THOMAS MCGREEVY, | ELLIOT PAUL, JOHN RODKER, ROBERT SAGE, | WILLIAM CARLOS WILLIAMS. | *with* | *LETTERS OF PROTEST* | BY | G. V. L. SLINGSBY AND VLADIMIR DIXON. | SHAKESPEARE AND COMPANY | SYLVIA BEACH | 12, RUE DE L'ODÉON—PARIS | [short rule] | M CM XX IX viii, 198 pp. 19.2 x 14.1 cm. 24 fr. Cream-colored paper covers, printed in black.

Colophon: 96 copies of this book have been printed on vergé d'Arches numbered 1–96. (These numbered copies measure 20 x 15 cm. and are twice as thick as the ordinary edition but otherwise identical in printing and binding.)

Contains, in addition to brief quotations from *Work in Progress* as it had been appearing in *transition,* a passage concerning Swift and blindness; p. 109, which was not later incorporated in *Finnegans Wake;* see E 7.*d*.

Sheets of this edition were later sold by Shakespeare and Company to both Faber & Faber, London, and New Directions, Norfolk, Connecticut, who bound them with inserted title pages.

The "Letters of Protest" are reputed to have been written by Joyce himself.

11. "A MUSTER FROM WORK IN PROGRESS" * 1929

transition | stories | Twenty-three stories from "transition" | selected and edited by | Eugene Jolas | and | Robert Sage | [publisher's device] | New York | Walter V. McKee | 1929

xii, 356 pp. 19 x 13 cm. $2.50. Decorated boards with a red cloth spine. Dust wrapper.

There was also a large paper issue of 100 copies: xiv, 354 pp. 24 x 16 cm. $10. Marbled boards with a green cloth spine.

Contains "A Muster from *Work in Progress,*" by James Joyce; pp. 177–91. Seven excerpts from *Finnegans Wake* as follows: FW 30–4, l. 29; 76, l. 33, to 78, l. 6; 65, ll. 5–33; 454, l. 26, to 455, l. 29; 413, ll. 3–24; 23, ll. 16–26; 74, ll. 13–19. These quotations, reprinted with revisions, were subsequently revised before publication of *Finnegans Wake.*

12. IMAGIST ANTHOLOGY 1930 1930

IMAGIST | ANTHOLOGY | 1930 | [line of dots] | *POEMS BY* | Richard Aldington | John Cournos | H. D. | John Gould Fletcher | F. S. Flint | Ford Madox Ford | James Joyce | D. H. Lawrence | William Carlos Williams | [line of dots] | *FOREWORDS BY* | Ford Madox Ford | Glenn Hughes | [line of dots] | CHATTO & WINDUS / LONDON | 1930 xx, 156 pp. 20 x 13.2 cm. *6s.* Yellow cloth, stamped in blue. Dust wrapper.

Contains From "Tales Told of Shem and Shaun; Three Fragments from Work in Progress" by James Joyce; pp. 121–2. This fragment (FW 417, l. 24, to 419, l. 10) was taken from *Tales Told of Shem and Shaun* (A 36).

American edition: New York, Covici, Friede, [1930]. 240 pp. 20.5 x 13.9 cm. $3.50. Light blue cloth with a buff paper label on spine. Dust wrapper. A note on p.[231] states: *The first edition of this book consists of one thousand copies.*

13. "A LITTLE CLOUD" 1930

This story from *Dubliners* is listed in the *Deutsches Bücherverzeichnis*, Leipzig, XIV (1932) (P–Z) 1562, as published with Yeats' "The Pot of Broth" and Lady Gregory's "The Rising of the Moon." Berlin, Weidmannsche Buchhandlung, Kleine 8vo, Short-Stories-Series, Vol. IV, p. 90. Not seen by the compilers.

14. "FROM ULYSSES" 1931

THE EUROPEAN | CARAVAN | AN ANTHOLOGY OF THE NEW SPIRIT IN | EUROPEAN LITERATURE | Compiled and Edited by | SAMUEL PUTNAM | MAIDA CASTELHUN DARNTON, GEORGE REAVEY | and | J. BRONOWSKI | With Special Introductions by | ANDRÉ BERGE, MASSIMO BONTEMPELLI, JEAN CASSOU | and | E. GIMÉNEZ CABELLERO | PART I | FRANCE, SPAIN, ENGLAND and IRELAND | BREWER, WARREN & PUTNAM | NEW YORK, 1931

xviii, 578 pp. 20.9 x 14 cm. $4. Black cloth, stamped in green. Dust wrapper.

Published November 13, 1931, in an edition of about 2,000 copies.

Contains "From *Ulysses*," by James Joyce; pp. 526–36. From the third episode; taken from the *Little Review* text.

15. "I HEAR AN ARMY" 1932

EZRA POUND | PROFILE [in red] | AN ANTHOLOGY COLLECTED IN MCMXXXI | MILAN MCMXXXII

148 pp. 20.4 x 15.5 cm. Gray paper covers.

Colophon: Edition privately printed for John Scheiwiller limited to 250 numbered copies.

Contains "I Hear an Army," by James Joyce; p. 19. *Chamber Music*, XXXVI.

16. "FROM JAMES JOYCE"** [1933]

THE CANTOS | of | EZRA POUND | Some Testimonials by | ERNEST HEMINGWAY | FORD MADOX FORD | T. S. ELIOT | HUGH WALPOLE | ARCHIBALD MACLEISH | JAMES JOYCE | and OTHERS | FARRAR & RINEHART, Inc. [device] PUBLISHERS: NEW YORK

24 pp. 19.7 x 13 cm. Cover title; stapled.

Issued early in 1933 in connection with the American publication of Pound's *A Draft of XXX Cantos* (1933).

Contains "IX. From James Joyce," dated September 15, 1932; pp. 12–13.

17. JOYCE & HUXLEY 1933

Sekibundo New English Texts [underlined] | JOYCE & HUXLEY | Edited With Notes | BY | K. OUCHI | *Professor of English in the Fukuoka Koto Gakko* | SEKIBUNDO | TOKYO

vi, 128 pp. 19.3 x 13.7 cm. Blue paper covers, printed in white.

Colophon: Issued March 5, 1933.

Contains "A Painful Case," "A Little Cloud," and "Eveline," by James Joyce; pp. 59–107. Apparently the first publication in English of these stories from *Dubliners* in Japan.

18. "A SERIES OF LETTERS REGARDING ULYSSES"** 1933

A CATALOGUE OF | RARE BOOKS, PICTURES, | MANUSCRIPTS & LETTERS | [photograph of portrait of Blake] | Portrait of Blake by Tatham (see item 3) | THE ULYSSES BOOKSHOP | AND THE ULYSSES PRESS LTD. | (DIRECTORS: JACOB AND DAVID SCHWARTZ) | NEW YORK AND LONDON | 21 WEST 51st STREET | NEW YORK CITY, N.Y. | MANAGER: LEO. SCHWARTZ TEL.: ELDORADO 5-7450

iv, 72 pp. 21.5 x 13.6 cm. Cover title; stapled.

The preface of this catalogue is dated November 15, 1933.

Contains "A Series of Letters Regarding *Ulysses*," by James Joyce;

pp. 28–9. A series of quotations from Joyce's correspondence with John Rodker, 1920–28.

19. "A LETTER FROM MR. JOYCE . . ."** 1934

[double title page, verso:] U [recto:] JAMES | JOYCE | LYSSES

xviii, 774 pp. 20.7 x 13.9 cm. $3.50. Cream-colored cloth, stamped in black and red. Dust wrapper.

The first authorized American edition of *Ulysses* published by Random House, New York, on January 25, 1934. For further details of this book see A 21.

Contains "A Letter from Mr. Joyce to the Publisher, Reprinted in this Edition by Permission of the Author," dated April 2, 1932; pp. xv–xvii.

20. ANGLO-IRISH SHORT STORIES 1936

THE KAWASE SERIES [underlined] | ANGLO-IRISH SHORT STORIES | LIAM O'FLAHERTY | JAMES JOYCE | LENNOX ROBINSON | AN PILIBIN | KAWASE & SONS

vi, 134 pp. 18.8 x 12.7 cm. Blue cloth, gilt stamped. Dust wrapper.

Colophon: Issued March 1, 1936.

Contains "The Sisters" and "A Painful Case," by James Joyce; pp. 41–68.

Apparently the first publication of "The Sisters" from *Dubliners* in English in Japan.

21. "ECCE PUER"* [1936]

The | NEW REPUBLIC | Anthology | 1915 : 1935 | Edited by | GROFF CONKLIN | Introduction by | BRUCE BLIVEN | [device] | DODGE PUBLISHING COMPANY | New York

[Note: The above is within a double-rule border.]

xlii, 566 pp. 21.2 x 14.4 cm. $3. Buff cloth, stamped in black and red. Dust wrapper.

"Published on October 5, 1936; approximately two thousand bound copies were sold, and there was a remainder of about twelve hundred sets of sheets." Gallup, *A Bibliographical Check-List of the Writings of T. S. Eliot*, New Haven, Yale University Library, 1947, B xxxv. Another copy, in blue cloth, stamped in black only, is presumably one of the remainder.

Contains "Ecce Puer, by James Joyce, November 30, 1932"; p. 438.

22. AS I WAS GOING DOWN SACKVILLE STREET* 1937

A PHANTASY IN FACT | [ornament] | AS I WAS | GOING DOWN | SACKVILLE | STREET | BY | OLIVER ST. J. GOGARTY | *Illustrated* | [ornament] | REYNAL & HITCHCOCK; NEW YORK

x, 342 pp. 23.8 x 15.8 cm. $3.50. Red cloth, stamped in black and gilt. Dust wrapper.

Published April 5, 1937. The total sales (1937–44) were about 5,700 copies.

An English edition published by Rich & Cowan, London, was also published in April 1937.

Contains a limerick about Lady Gregory, ascribed to James Joyce; p. 294. Gogarty reprints this limerick in his *Mourning Became Mrs. Spendlove* (1948).

23. JAMES JOYCE [1939]

James Joyce | *by* | *Herbert Gorman* | *Illustrated with Photographs* | *Farrar & Rinehart, Inc.* | *New York Toronto*
[Note: The above is within a triple-rule border.]

vi, 362 pp. Illus. 22.8 x 15.2 cm. $3.50. Green cloth, gilt stamped. Dust wrapper.

Published February 15, 1940, in an edition of 2,490 copies. The copyright date is 1939.

The English edition of this biography was published in January 1941 by John Lane, The Bodley Head, London, reset and illustrated with photomontages instead of photographs as in the American edition: vi, 354 pp. Illus. 21.5 x 13.7 cm. Red cloth, stamped in yellow. Dust wrapper.

A new American edition with an additional page of text was published by Rinehart, New York, on December 31, 1948, in an edition of 2,000 copies.

Contains the following items by James Joyce:

** English version of Ode III, 13, from Horace; pp. 45–6.
** English version of Verlaine's "Les Sanglots Longues"; p. 59.
Excerpts from *Ibsen's New Drama;* pp. 65–8.
** A letter to Henrik Ibsen, dated March, 1901; pp. 69–70.
* Excerpts from "The Day of the Rabblement"; pp. 71–3. These excerpts contain three errors in transcription.
From *A Portrait of the Artist as a Young Man;* p. 75.
Excerpts from "James Clarence Mangan"; pp. 77–9, 80.
** A letter to his mother, dated February 2, 1903; p. 93.
** Excerpts from his Paris notebook, dated February and March, 1903; pp. 95–9.
* *The Holy Office;* pp. 138–41.
** A letter to Grant Richards, dated January 16, 1905; pp. 141–2.
** Remark to a friend concerning Trieste; p. 143.
** Excerpts from letters to his brother Stanislaus, one dated July 1905; pp. 143–4.
** Letters to Grant Richards, dated December 3, 1905, February 28, March 13, May 5, May 13, June 10, June 16, and July 9, 1906; pp. 146, 147–57.
** Excerpts from letters to his brother Stanislaus, 1906; pp. 163, 166–7.
** Excerpt from a letter to his brother Stanislaus, dated August 14, 1906; pp. 169–70.
** Letters to Grant Richards, dated September 23 and October 22, 1906; pp. 170, 173.
** Excerpt from a letter to his brother Stanislaus, 1906; p. 171.
** Excerpts from letters to his brother Stanislaus, dated September 30 and November 13, 1906, and February 6, 1907; p. 176.
** Excerpts from letters to his brother Stanislaus, dated August 19 and 31, October and November 1906 and later; pp. 178, 179, 180, 181, 182, 188.
* Brief excerpts from articles in *Il Piccolo della Sera,* Trieste; p. 194.
** A letter to his sister Poppie, undated; pp. 196–7.

** Excerpts from letters to and from his brother Stanislaus, undated, December 1909, February and March 12, 1910; pp. 197–8, 200–1, 202, 203.
** A letter to Elkin Mathews, dated April 4, 1910; pp. 203–4.
** A letter to Maunsel, Dublin, dated July 10, 1904; pp. 204–5.
A letter to the press, dated August 18, 1911; pp. 206–8.
** Excerpt from a letter to his brother Stanislaus, undated; pp. 210–11.
** A letter to George Roberts, dated August 21, 1912; pp. 213–14.
** Excerpt from a letter to his brother Stanislaus, *c.* August 1912; pp. 215–16.
* *Gas from a Burner;* pp. 217–19.
** Letters to Grant Richards, dated January 8, undated, and February 3, 1914; pp. 222–3.
* Conversation with Georges Borach; p. 224.
** "Epilogue to Ibsen's *Ghosts,*" dated April 1934; footnote, pp. 226–7.
** Remarks to friends in Zurich; p. 234.
** A parody of "Mr. Dooley"; pp. 240–1.
** Five humorous poems (four of them limericks); pp. 248–9.
** A letter to Claud Sykes, dated January 2, 1918; p. 250.
"The C.G. Is Not Literary"; p. 256.
* Program notes for the English Players; pp. 258–9.
** "The Right Man in the Wrong Place"; p. 262.
** Excerpts from letters to his brother Stanislaus, undated, July 25, end of August, two days later, 1920, undated; pp. 273, 274, 275.
** Remark to Valery Larbaud about the Unknown Soldier; p. 276.
** Parody of "Molly Brannigan"; pp. 282–3.
** Excerpt from a letter to his brother Stanislaus, dated March 20, 1922; p. 291.
* Verse composed apropos of the London publication of *Anna Livia Plurabelle* and *Haveth Childers Everywhere;* pp. 343–4.
* A translation into French of James Stephens' "Stephen's Green"; pp. 344–5.
** A translation from German into English of a poem by Gottfried Keller; p. 345.
** Remark concerning John Sullivan; p. 346.

24. IN MEMORIAM JAMES JOYCE** [1941]

IN MEMORIAM | JAMES JOYCE | HERAUSGEGEBEN VON | C. GIEDION-WELCKER | FRETZ & WASMUTH VERLAG AG. ZÜRICH

56 pp. Illus. 24.3 x 16.4 cm. 4.50 Swiss fr. Bound in stiff coated green paper, printed in gilt. Published May 1941.

Two editions of this pamphlet exist. In one all captions, titles, and articles, with the exception of the address by Lord Derwent and Joyce's two poems, are in German. In the other all captions and titles, plus an article by Mme Carola Giedion-Welcker and the two items noted above, are in English.

Contains a letter to the Canton President, by James Joyce, dated December 20, 1940; pp. 51–2. Also contains reprints of "Alone" and "Bahnhofstrasse" from *Pomes Penyeach;* p. 53.

25. LETTER TO CARLO LINATI** 1944

JAMES JOYCE | ESULI | (1918) | ROSA E BALLO EDITORI—MILANO | 1944

xii, 150 pp. 15.8 x 11.9 cm. Collana Teatro Moderno, a Cura di Paolo Grassi [1]. Translated by Carlo Linati.

Published in July 1944.

This translation of *Exiles* contains a letter written in Italian from Joyce to Carlo Linati, Trieste, December 10, 1919; pp. ix–x.

26. OUT OF THIS CENTURY** 1946

out | of | this | century | the informal | memoirs of peggy guggenheim | the dial press | 1946 | new york

x, 366 pp. 20.3 x 13.3 cm. $3.75. Dark blue cloth, stamped in yellow. Dust wrapper.

Published March 26, 1946, in an edition of 6,000 copies.

Contains a poem ascribed to James Joyce, written to Mrs. Herbert Gorman about Peggy Guggenheim and her husband John Holm; p. 130.

27. LIFE AND THE DREAM** 1947

Life and | the Dream | MARY COLUM | [device] | DOUBLEDAY & COMPANY, INC. | *Garden City, N. Y. 1947* xiv, 466 pp. 21.1 x 14.4 cm. $3.50. Brown cloth, stamped in gilt and green. Dust wrapper.

Published March 20, 1947, in an edition of 6,500 copies.

Contains verses ascribed to James Joyce; p. 395.

28. "FROM A BANNED WRITER TO A BANNED SINGER"* [1948]

TURNSTILE | ONE | *A Literary Miscellany from* | THE NEW STATESMAN AND NATION | *Edited by* | V. S. PRITCHETT | [device] | TURNSTILE PRESS | 10 Great Turnstile, London, W. C. 1.

x, 254 pp. 21.3 x 13.4 cm. 10*s*. 6*d*. Gray cloth, stamped in red and gold. Dust wrapper.

Published in March 1948.

Contains "From a Banned Writer to a Banned Singer," by James Joyce; pp. 10–13. See also C 81, 85.

29. JAMES JOYCE 1949

[double title page, verso:] JAMES [recto:] JOYCE | SA VIE | SON ŒUVRE | SON RAYONNEMENT | OCTOBRE–NOVEMBRE | 1949 | LA HUNE | 170, BOULEVARD SAINT-GERMAIN | PARIS-VI e

[128] pp. Illus. 21 x 16.3 cm. 400 fr. Green paper covers, printed in blue and black. The front cover contains a photograph of a Dublin lamp post and street sign; the back cover, a map of Dublin.

Introductory note p. [5] signed *Bernard Gheerbrant.*

The colophon states that 1,500 copies were printed, of which 1 to 30 were numbered and contained an etching in two colors by Johny Friedlander representing the arms of the Joyce family. These 30 copies sold for 1,500 fr. each.

Contains the following items by James Joyce:

** A French translation of a letter to Lady Gregory, dated November 22, 1902; No. 46.

* Excerpt from a French translation of "From a Banned Writer to a Banned Singer"; No. [104].

** A French translation of an excerpt from a letter to W. B. Yeats, dated September 5, 1932; No. 136.

** The French translations of five "Epiphanies," which are apparently Nos. 3, 7, 10, 15, 17, and 11 (in English MS facsimile) in order printed; No. 159.

** A French translation of excerpts from reviews by Joyce from the *Dublin Daily Express;* Nos. 165, 166.

** A French translation of the beginning of an unpublished manuscript of *Exiles;* No. 240.

30. "AD-WRITER"** 1949

A | JAMES JOYCE | YEARBOOK | *Edited by* | *Maria Jolas* | 1949 | *Transition Workshop* | Transition Press | Paris

200 pp. Illus. 19.5 x 14.1 cm. $3.50. Stiff cream-colored decorated covers, printed in green and black.

Colophon: Edition limited to 1,000 [numbered] copies including 50 bound copies on Renage pur fil. Printed July 25, 1949.

Contains "Ad-Writer," ascribed to James Joyce; p. 170.

31. I HEAR YOU CALLING ME* [1949]

LILY MC CORMACK | I Hear You | Calling Me | [coat of arms] | THE BRUCE PUBLISHING COMPANY | MILWAUKEE

[viii], 204 pp. Illus. 20.2 x 14 cm. $2.75. Gray cloth, stamped in green. Dust wrapper.

Published November 15, 1949, in an edition of 23,500 copies.

Contains a paragraph from a letter from James Joyce to John McCormack written in 1920; p. 116. See also C 103.

32. JAMES JOYCE'S DUBLIN** 1950

PATRICIA HUTCHINS | James Joyce's Dublin | THE GREY WALLS PRESS

120 pp. Illus. 25 x 18.6 cm. 15*s*. Green cloth, gilt stamped. Dust wrapper.

Published in London, September 17, 1950.

Contains a limerick about Lady Gregory which first appeared in Gogarty's *As I Was Going Down Sackville Street* (1937) (see B 22); p. 83. Quotes and reproduces letters from Joyce to his aunt Mrs. Josephine Murray, previously unpublished.

Reviewed by Stanislaus Joyce in *Partisan Review*, New York, XIX.1 (Jan–Feb 1952) [103]–109.

C. *Contributions by James Joyce to Periodicals and Newspapers*

1. IBSEN'S NEW DRAMA. *Fortnightly Review*, London, N.S. LXVII.400 (Apr 1, 1900) 575–90.

A review of *When We Dead Awaken*, by Henrik Ibsen, translated by William Archer. Signed *James A. Joyce* . Separately reprinted in 1930 (A 40).

2. JAMES CLARENCE MANGAN. *Saint Stephen's*, Dublin, I.6 (May 1902) 116–18.

Signed, *James A. Joyce*. Separately reprinted in 1930 (A 39). Reprinted in *National Student*, Dublin, 114 (Mar 1952) 9–12.

3. GEORGE MEREDITH. *Daily Express*, Dublin, December 11, 1902.

A review of *George Meredith: An Essay towards Appreciation*, by Walter Jerrold. Not reprinted. Unsigned.

4. AN IRISH POET. *Daily Express*, Dublin, December 11, 1902.

A review of *Poems and Ballads of William Rooney*. Partially reprinted in French translation in Gheerbrant (B 29), No. 165. Unsigned.

5. TO-DAY AND TO-MORROW IN IRELAND. *Daily Express*, Dublin, January 29, 1903.

A review of *To-day and To-morrow in Ireland*, by Stephen Gwynn. Not reprinted. Unsigned.

6. A SUAVE PHILOSOPHY. *Daily Express*, Dublin, February 6, 1903.

A review of *The Soul of a People*, by H. Fielding Hall. Not reprinted. Unsigned.

7. AN EFFORT AT PRECISION IN THINKING. *Daily Express*, Dublin, February 6, 1903.

A review of *Colloquies of Common People*, reported by James Austie [*sic*], K.C. The correct surname of the author is Anstie. Not reprinted. Unsigned.

8. COLONIAL VERSES. *Daily Express*, Dublin, February 6, 1903.

A review of *Songs of an English Esau*, by Clive Phillipps Wolley. Not reprinted. Unsigned.

9. CATALINA. *Speaker*, London, N.S. VII.181 (Mar 21, 1903) 615.

A review of *Catalina*, by Henrik Ibsen, translated into French by the Vicomte de Colleville and F. de Zepelin. Not reprinted. Unsigned.

10. THE SOUL OF IRELAND. *Daily Express*, Dublin, March 26, 1903, p. 11.

A review of *Poets and Dreamers*, by Lady Gregory. Signed *J.J.* Partially reprinted in French translation in Gheerbrant (B 29), No. 166.

11. THE MOTOR DERBY: INTERVIEW WITH THE FRENCH CHAMPION. *Irish Times*, Dublin, April 7, 1903.

An interview with the French driver Henri Fournier about the forthcoming Gordon Bennett Cup Race in Ireland. Not reprinted. Unsigned.

12. [A review of] *A Ne'er-Do-Well*, by Valentine Caryl [pseudonym of Valentina Hawtrey]. *Daily Express*, Dublin, September 3, 1903. Not reprinted. Unsigned.

13. ARISTOTLE ON EDUCATION. *Daily Express*, Dublin, September 3, 1903.

A review of *Aristotle on Education*, edited by John Burnet. Not reprinted. Unsigned.

14. [A review of] *The Adventures of Prince Aga Mirza*, by Aquila Kempster. *Daily Express*, Dublin, September 17, 1903. Not reprinted. Unsigned.

15. [A review of] *The Mettle of the Pasture*, by James Lane Allen. *Daily Express*, Dublin, September 17, 1903. Not reprinted. Unsigned.

16. A PEEP INTO HISTORY. *Daily Express*, Dublin, September 17, 1903.

A review of *The Popish Plot*, by John Pollock. Not reprinted. Unsigned.

17. MR. ARNOLD GRAVES' NEW WORK. *Daily Express*, Dublin, October 1, 1903.

A review of *Clytemnæstra: A Tragedy*, by Arnold F. Graves. Not reprinted. Unsigned.

18. A FRENCH RELIGIOUS NOVEL. *Daily Express*, Dublin, October 1, 1903.

A review of *The House of Sin*, by Marcelle Tintyre [*sic*], translated by A. Smyth. The correct surname of the author is Tinayre. Not reprinted. Unsigned.

19. UNEQUAL VERSE. *Daily Express*, Dublin, October 1, 1903.
A review of *Ballads and Legends*, by Frederick Langbridge. Not reprinted. Unsigned.

20. A NEGLECTED POET. *Daily Express*, Dublin, October 15, 1903.
A review of *George Crabbe*, by Alfred Ainger. Not reprinted. Unsigned.

21. MR. MASON'S NOVELS. *Daily Express*, Dublin, October 15, 1903.
A review of *The Courtship of Morrice Buckler*, *The Philanderers*, and *Miranda of the Balcony*, by A. E. W. Mason. Not reprinted. Unsigned.

22. THE BRUNO PHILOSOPHY. *Daily Express*, Dublin, October 30, 1903.
A review of *Giordano Bruno*, by J. Lewis McIntyre. Not reprinted. Unsigned.

23. HUMANISM. *Daily Express*, Dublin, November 12, 1903.
A review of *Humanism: Philosophical Essays*, by F. S. C. Schiller. The correct name of the author is F. C. S. Schiller. Not reprinted. Unsigned.

24. SHAKESPEARE EXPLAINED! *Daily Express*, Dublin, November 12, 1903.
A review of *Shakespeare Studied in Eight Plays*, by Hon. A[lbert] S. [G.] Canning. Not reprinted. Unsigned.

25. [A review of] *Borlase and Son*, by T. Baron Russell. *Daily Express*, Dublin, November 19, 1903. Not reprinted. Unsigned.

26. SONG. *Saturday Review*, London, XCVII.2533 (May 14, 1904) 619.
Chamber Music, XXIV. Signed *James A. Joyce*.

27. [O SWEETHEART] *Speaker*, London, N.S. X.252 (Jul 30, 1904) 408.
Chamber Music, XVIII. Signed *James A. Joyce*. Untitled but listed in index as "O Sweetheart."

28. SONG. *Dana*, Dublin, 4 (Aug 1904) 124.
Chamber Music, VII. Signed *James A. Joyce*.

29. THE SISTERS. *Irish Homestead*, Dublin, X.33 (Aug 13, 1904) 676–7.
The text of this story is shorter and differs considerably from the text in *Dubliners*, 1914. Signed *Stephen Daedalus*.

30. EVELINE. *Irish Homestead*, Dublin, x.37 (Sept 10, 1904) 761.

The text of this story differs slightly from the text in *Dubliners*, 1914. Signed *Stephen Daedalus.*

31. A WISH. *Speaker*, London, N.S. XI.262 (Oct 8, 1904) 36.

Chamber Music, VI, with ll. 2 and 3 transposed. Signed *James A. Joyce.*

32. AFTER THE RACE. *Irish Homestead*, Dublin, x.51 (Dec 17, 1904) 1038–9.

The text of this story is substantially the same as the text in *Dubliners*, 1914. Signed *Stephen Daedalus.*

33. IL FENIANISMO. L'ULTIMO FENIANO. *Il Piccolo della Sera*, Trieste, XXVI (Mar 22, 1907) 1.

Text in Italian. Not reprinted.

34. HOME RULE MAGGIORENNE. *Il Piccolo della Sera*, Trieste, XXVI (May 19, 1907) 1.

Text in Italian. Not reprinted.

35. L'IRLANDA ALLA SBARRA. *Il Piccolo della Sera*, Trieste, XXVI (Sept 16, 1907) 1.

Text in Italian. Not reprinted.

35A. OSCAR WILDE: IL POETA DI SALOME. *Il Piccolo della Sera*, Trieste, XXVIII (Mar 24, 1909).

Text in Italian. Not reprinted. Not seen by the compilers. See E 8.

36. LA BATTAGLIA FRA BERNARD SHAW E LA CENSURA. "BLANCO POSNET SMASCHERATO." *Il Piccolo della Sera*, Trieste, XXVIII (Sept 5, 1909) 3.

By a typographical error the author's name appears as James Yoyce. Text in Italian. Not reprinted.

37. SONG. *Irish Homestead*, Dublin, XVII.38 (Sept 17, 1910) 785.

Chamber Music, I.

38. LA COMETA DELL' "HOME RULE." *Il Piccolo della Sera*, Trieste, XXIX (Dec 22, 1910) 1.

Text in Italian. Not reprinted.

39. AUTHOR AND PUBLISHER IN IRELAND. *Northern Whig*, Belfast, August 26, 1911.

A letter which subsequently became the text of *A Curious His-*

tory. Does not print the disputed passages of *Dubliners*. See C 40, below.

40. DUBLINERS. TO THE EDITOR OF SINN FEIN. *Sinn Fein*, Dublin, II.83 (O.S. 275) (Sept 2, 1911) 2.

Same as C 39, above, except that it prints the disputed passages of *Dubliners*. Reprinted in the *Egoist* (C 44 below); separately reprinted as *A Curious History* (B 5) and also reprinted in Gorman, 1939, pp. 206–8.

41. L'OMBRA DI PARNELL. *Il Piccolo della Sera*, Trieste, XXXI (May 16, 1912) 1.

Text in Italian. Not reprinted.

42. IL MIRAGGIO DEL PESCATORE DI ARAN. LA VALVOLA DELL'INGHILTERRA IN CASO DI GUERRA. *Il Piccolo della Sera*, Trieste, XXXI (Sept 5, 1912) 2.

Text in Italian. Not reprinted.

43. WATCHING THE NEEDLEBOATS AT SAN SABBA. *Saturday Review*, London, CXVI.3021 (Sept 20, 1913) 366.

Included in *Pomes Penyeach*.

44. A CURIOUS HISTORY. *Egoist*, London, I.2 (Jan 15, 1914) 26–7.

A series of letters by Joyce, introduced by Ezra Pound, which recount his difficulties in publishing *Dubliners*. Separately reprinted as *A Curious History* (B 5) and also reprinted in Gorman, 1939, pp. 206–8.

45. I HEAR AN ARMY. *Glebe*, New York, I.5 (Feb 1914) 40.

Chamber Music, XXXVI. This entire issue of *Glebe* is devoted to "Des Imagistes; an Anthology." The second appearance of Joyce in America. (For the first appearance see F 1). See also B 4.

46. A PORTRAIT OF THE ARTIST AS A YOUNG MAN.

A Portrait ran serially in the *Egoist*, London, from Vol. I, No. 3, to Vol. II, No. 9 (Feb 2, 1914, to Sept 1, 1915), in 25 installments. There was a hiatus of five numbers, Vol. I, Nos. 18–22, when Joyce was unable to send the manuscript from Trieste to London, and an installment was not included in Vol. II, No. 5 (May 1, 1915), which was a special Imagist issue. The text, allowing for printer's errors, is substantially the same as the text of the first edition (1916), with the exception of the opening pages of Chapter III, p. 115, l. 9, to p. 116, l. 5, which is omitted from the *Egoist* serialization.

Egoist, London, I.3 (Feb 2, 1914) 50–3. This installment appears in the first edition, New York, Huebsch, 1916 (H), and all subsequent separate American printings (except the Signet edition, 1948) as pp. 1–14. Following is a list of the other installments in the *Egoist*.

I.4 (Feb 16, 1914) 70–2 (H 14–26).
I.5 (Mar 2, 1914) 93–6 (H 26–41).
I.6 (Mar 16, 1914) 107–8 (H 41–8).
I.7 (Apr 1, 1914) 132–4 (H 48–55).
I.8 (Apr 15, 1914) 151–3 (H 55–64).
I.9 (May 1, 1914) 165–6 (H 65–73).
I.10 (May 15, 1914) 187–9 (H 73–80).
I.11 (June 1, 1914) 210–11 (H 80–7).
I.12 (June 15, 1914) 231–3 (H 87–96).
I.13 (Jul 1, 1914) 248–51 (H 97–108).
I.14 (Jul 15, 1914) 273–4 (H 108–14).
I.15 (Aug 1, 1914) 289–91 (H 115–27).
I.16 (Aug 15, 1914) 310–13 (H 127–45).
I.17 (Sept 1, 1914) 327–32 (H 145–69).
I.23 (Dec 1, 1914) 438–9 (H 170–8).
I.24 (Dec 15, 1914) 456–8 (H 178–90).
II.1 (Jan 1, 1915) 7–9 (H 190–201).
II.2 (Feb 1, 1915) 25–8 (H 202–14).
II.3 (Mar 1, 1915) 42–5 (H 214–26).
II.4 (Apr 1, 1915) 54–6 (H 226–39).
II.6 (June 1, 1915) 93–6 (H 239–53).
II.7 (Jul 1, 1915) 107–9 (H 253–63).
II.8 (Aug 2, 1915) 127–30 (H 263–81).
II.9 (Sept 1, 1915) 144–7 (H 281–99).

47. THE BOARDING HOUSE. A LITTLE CLOUD. *Smart Set*, New York, XLVI.1 (May 1915) 93–7, 129–36.

Reprinted from the English edition of *Dubliners*, 1914.

48. SIMPLES. TUTTO È SCIOLTO. FLOOD. A FLOWER GIVEN TO MY DAUGHTER. NIGHTPIECE. *Poetry*, Chicago, X.2 (May 1917) 72–5.

Included in *Pomes Penyeach*. The text of the second poem differs substantially from the final text; the others are approximately the same.

49. FROM JAMES JOYCE. *Little Review,* New York, IV.2 (June 1917) 26.

A letter to the editors promising to send a contribution. Not reprinted.

50. "DUBLINERS." *Evening Mail,* New York, LXXXI.177 (Jul 28, 1917) 7.

A reprint of *A Curious History;* see Nos. C 39, 40, and 44. There may be other and earlier publications of this item in American newspapers.

51. ON THE BEACH AT FONTANA. ALONE. SHE WEEPS OVER RAHOON. *Poetry,* Chicago, XI.2 (Nov 1917) 70–1.

Included in *Pomes Penyeach.* The text of the third poem, second stanza, second line, differs from the final text; the other poems are approximately the same. "She Weeps over Rahoon" was reprinted in the *Literary Digest,* New York, LVI.2 (Jan 12, 1918) 45.

52. EXTRACT FROM "IL MARZOCCO." *Egoist,* London, V.2 (Feb 1918) 30.

The translation from Italian of this highly favorable review of *A Portrait of the Artist as a Young Man* was made by Joyce at the request of Miss Harriet Weaver.

53. ULYSSES.

The *Little Review,* New York, between March 1918 and December 1920, published serially 13 and part of the 14th of the 18 episodes of *Ulysses.* In all, 23 installments appeared before publication was stopped by action brought by the Society for the Suppression of Vice. The January and May 1919 and January and July–August 1920 numbers were banned by the United States Post Office.

Little Review, New York, IV (incorrectly numbered V). 11 (Mar 1918) 3–22. This installment appears in the first authorized American edition, New York, Random House, 1934 (RH) and the Modern Library Giant Edition as pp. 4–24.

The other installments are as follows:

IV (incorrectly numbered V).12 (Apr 1918) 32–45 (RH 25–37).
V.1 (May 1918) 31–45 (RH 38–51).
V (incorrectly numbered IV).2 (June 1918) 39–52 (RH 54–69).
V.3 (Jul 1918) 37–49 (RH 70–85).

v.5 (Sept 1918) 15–37 (RH 86–114).
v.6 (Oct 1918) 26–51 (RH 115–48).
v.9 (Jan 1919) 27–50 (RH 149–76).
v.10–11 (Feb–Mar 1919) 58–62 (RH 176–81).
v.12 (incorrectly numbered 11) (Apr 1919) 30–43 (RH 182–95).
vi.1 (May 1919) 17–35 (RH 195–215).
vi.2 (June 1919) 34–45 (RH 216–28).
vi.3 (Jul 1919) 28–47 (RH 228–51).
vi.4 (Aug 1919) 41–64 (RH 252–76).
vi.5 (Sept 1919) 46–55 (RH 276–86).
vi.7 (Nov 1919) 38–54 (RH 287–308).
vi.8 (Dec 1919) 50–60 (RH 308–21).
vi.9 (Jan 1920) 53–61 (RH 321–32).
vi.10 (Mar 1920) 54–60 (RH 332–9).
vi.11 (Apr 1920) 43–50 (RH 340–7).
vii.1 (May–June 1920) 61–72 (RH 347–58).
vii.2 (Jul–Aug 1920) 42–58 (RH 358–76).
vii.3 (Sept–Dec 1920) 81–92 (RH 377–88).

54. ULYSSES.

The *Egoist*, London, between January and December 1919, when it ceased publication, published about three and a half episodes of *Ulysses* in five numbers as follows:

vi.1 (Jan–Feb 1919) 11–14 (RH 25–37).
vi.2 (Mar–Apr 1919) 26–30 (RH 38–51).
vi.3 (Jul 1919) 42–6 (RH 86–99).
vi.4 (Sept 1919) 56–60 (RH 99–114).
vi.5 (Dec 1919) 74–8 (RH 216–26).

55. BAHNHOFSTRASSE. *Anglo-French Review*, London, ii.1 (Aug 15, 1919) 44.

Included in *Pomes Penyeach*.

56. A MEMORY OF THE PLAYERS IN A MIRROR AT MIDNIGHT. *Poesia*, Milan, i.1 (Apr 15, 1920) 27.

Included in *Pomes Penyeach*.

57. A MEMORY OF THE PLAYERS IN A MIRROR AT MIDNIGHT. *Dial*, New York, lxix.1 (Jul 1920) 26.

Included in *Pomes Penyeach*.

58. JOTTINGS. *Evening Mail,* Dublin, August 27, 1922.

The columnist "A Man about Town" in describing Barney Kiernan's public house quotes (incorrectly) from *Ulysses* Joyce's curse on the place (RH 307).

59. JAMES JOYCE'S FIRST LITERARY EFFORT: THE DAY OF THE RABBLEMENT. *New York Tribune*, New York (Dec 24, 1922) 19.

Reprinted from Mary Colum's copy by Burton Rascoe.

60. THE DAY OF THE RABBLEMENT: HOW JAMES JOYCE BROKE WITH THE IRISH RENAISSANCE. *Playboy*, New York, II.1 (First Quarter 1923) 41.

61. POEMS. *Querschnitt,* Frankfurt a.M., III.3/4 (Fall 1923) 157–9.

Chamber Music, XII, XV, XXVI, XXIX, and XXXVI.

62. FROM WORK IN PROGRESS. *transatlantic review,* Paris, I.4 (Apr 1924) 215–23 (FW 383–99).

The first published fragment of the work that was published in 1939 (New York, Viking; London, Faber & Faber) as *Finnegans Wake* (FW). The pagination in the New York and London editions is the same. It was Ford Madox Ford, editor of *transatlantic review,* who gave Joyce's unfinished work the title "Work in Progress."

63. LETTER TO ERNEST WALSH. *This Quarter*, Paris, I.1 (Spring 1925) 219.

A letter written in reply to the editor's request for a contribution about Ezra Pound. Not reprinted.

64. FRAGMENT OF AN UNPUBLISHED WORK. *Criterion,* London, III.12 (Jul 1925) 498–510 (FW 104–25).

65. A NEW UNNAMED WORK.

Between September 1925 and September 1926 *Two Worlds,* New York, edited by Samuel Roth, published five installments of "Work in Progress," reprinted from European publications. The reprints in *Two Worlds* were unauthorized by Joyce; they ceased because no further fragments of "Work in Progress" were available for Roth to reprint. The five installments are as follows:

I.1 (Sept 1925) 45–54 (FW 104–25). Reprinted from *Criterion,* July 1925.

I.2 (Dec 1925) 111–14 (FW 30–4). Reprinted from *Contact Collection of Contemporary Writers*, Paris, Contact Editions, 1925 (B 7).
I.3 (Mar 1926) 347–60 (FW 196–216). Reprinted from *Navire d'Argent*, Paris, October 1925.
I.4 (June 1926) 545–60 (FW 169–95). Reprinted from *This Quarter*, Milan, Autumn–Winter 1925–26.
II.5 (Sept 1926) 35–40 (FW 383–99). Reprinted from *transatlantic review*, Paris, April 1924.

66. FROM WORK IN PROGRESS. *Navire d'Argent*, Paris, I [i.e., II].5 (Oct 1925) 59–74 (FW 196–216).

67. EXTRACT FROM WORK IN PROGRESS. *This Quarter*, Milan, I.2 (Autumn–Winter 1925–26) 108–23 (FW 169–95).

68. ULYSSES.

Two Worlds Monthly, New York, reprinted 14 episodes of *Ulysses* in a bowdlerized form in 12 installments. These reprints were unauthorized by Joyce. The entire run of *Two Worlds Monthly*, Vols. I–III (Jul 1926–Oct 1927), with four numbers in each volume, was later issued in two bound volumes with an extra preface by the editor Samuel Roth. Vol. III.4 was not issued separately, i.e., apart from the bound volume. This unauthorized serialization of *Ulysses* resulted in considerable public indignation and provoked the "International Protest" signed by 167 artists and writers and printed in *transition*, Paris, I (Apr 1927), 156–8, and reprinted in Gorman, 1939, pp. 309–12. Joyce's American legal representatives obtained an injunction against Samuel Roth and Two Worlds Publishing Company on December 27, 1928, over a year after *Two Worlds Monthly* had ceased publication. The 12 installments are as follows:

I.1 [Jul 1926] 93–128 (RH 4–51).
I.2 [Aug 1926] 205–52 (RH 54–114).
I.3 [Sept 1926] 353–76 (RH 115–48).
I.4 [Oct 1926] 473–98 (RH 149–81).
II.1 (Dec 1926) 93–118 (RH 182–215).
II.2 (Jan 1927) 213–39 (RH 216–51).
II.3 (Feb 1927) 311–57 (RH 252–312).
II.4 (Mar 1927) 425–76 (RH 312–76).

III.1 (Apr 1927) 101–16 (RH 377–95).
III.2 (May–June 1927) 169–78 (RH 395–405).
III.3 (Sept 1927) 195–204 (RH 405–17).
III.4 [Oct 1927] 233–6 (RH 417–21).

69. LETTER FROM JAMES JOYCE TO CARLO LINATI, 19 DECEMBER, 1919. *Il Convegno*, Milan, VII.11–12 (Nov–Dec 1926) 818–19.
A photographic reproduction. Not reprinted.

70. WORK IN PROGRESS.
Between April 1927 and April–May 1938 *transition*, Paris, ran serially all of Part I, the first three chapters of Part II, and all of Part III of *Finnegans Wake*. In each case where *transition* duplicated a previous publication there was an extensive revision of the text; the text was usually revised again before final publication in *Finnegans Wake*.

OPENING PAGES OF A WORK IN PROGRESS. *transition*, Paris, 1 (Apr 1927) 9–30 (FW 3–29).

CONTINUATION OF A WORK IN PROGRESS. *transition*, Paris, 2 (May 1927) 94–107 (FW 30–47).

3 (June 1927) 32–50 (FW 48–74).
4 (Jul 1927) 46–65 (FW 75–103).
5 (Aug 1927) 15–31 (FW 104–25).
6 (Sept 1927) 87–106 f. (FW 126–68).
7 (Oct 1927) 34–56 (FW 169–95).
8 (Nov 1927) 17–35 (FW 196–216).
11 (Feb 1928) 7–18 (FW 282–304).
12 (Mar 1928) 7–27 (FW 403–28).
13 (Summer 1928) 5–32 (FW 429–73).
15 (Feb 1929) 195–238 (FW 474–554).
18 (Nov 1929) 211–36 (FW 555–90).
22 (Feb 1933) 49–76 (FW 219–59).

WORK IN PROGRESS. *transition*, Paris, 23 (Jul 1935) 109–29 (FW 260–75, 304–8).
26 (Feb 1937) 35–52 (FW 309–31).

FRAGMENT FROM WORK IN PROGRESS. *transition*, Paris, 27 (Apr–May 1938) 59–78 (FW 338–55).

71. LETTRE D'ENVOI. AU DIRECTEUR DES FEUILLES LIBRES. *Les Feuilles Libres*, Paris, N.S. 8ième année, 45–6 (June 1927) 173.
Text in French. Not reprinted.

72. LETTER TO THE EDITOR, 10 FEBRUARY, 1928. *Revue Nouvelle*, Paris, IV.38–9 (Jan–Feb 1928) 61.
Not reprinted.

73. MR. JOYCE DIRECTS AN IRISH PROSE BALLET. *transition*, Paris, 15 (Feb 1929) 126–34.
In this article about *Work in Progress* the author Robert McAlmon quotes a passage (p. 129) that did not appear in the final work. Harry Levin first called attention to this fact.

74. LETTER. *Solaria*, Florence, IV.3–4 (Mar–Apr 1929) 47.
A letter from Joyce praising the work of Italo Svevo is included in a section entitled "Omaggio a Svevo." In Italian.

75. LETTER. *Little Review*, New York and Paris, XII.2 (May 1929) 50–1.
A letter in answer to a questionnaire, declining to answer the questions.

76. LA CAVALCATA AL MARE. *Solaria*, Florence, IV.9–10 (Sept–Oct 1929) 3–16.
A translation of J. M. Synge's *Riders to the Sea*, by Joyce and Nicoló Vidacovich. In Italian.

77. THE LYRICS OF JAMES JOYCE. *Poetry*, Chicago, XXVI.4 (Jul 1930) 206–13.
In this article by Morton Dauwen Zabel three lyrics from *Pomes Penyeach* are reprinted, "Tilly" for the first time in America.

78. SARTOR RESARTUS. *This Quarter*, Paris, III.1 (Jul–Aug 1930) 141.
In a long article on Stuart Gilbert's *James Joyce's Ulysses* the author Edward Titus quotes 10 lines from *The Holy Office*.

79. FROM WORK IN PROGRESS. *New Experiment*, Cambridge, England, 7 (Spring 1931) 27–9 (FW 3–29).

80. GESPRÄCHE MIT JAMES JOYCE. *Die neue Zürcher Zeitung*, Zurich, May 3, 1931.
This article by Georges Borach contains extremely important

quotations from Joyce on the subject of his esthetics. Reprinted in *Omnibus; Almanach auf das Jahr 1932*, Berlin, etc., 1932, pp. 141–2.

81. FROM A BANNED WRITER TO A BANNED SINGER. *New Statesman and Nation*, London, N.S. III.53 (Feb 27, 1932) 260–1.

A tribute to John Sullivan, the Irish tenor. Reprinted in *Turnstile One* (B 28).

82. LES VERTS DE JACQUES. *transition*, Paris, 21 (Mar 1932) 257.

A translation into French by Joyce of the poem "Stephen's Green," by James Stephens. Reprinted in Gorman, 1939, pp. 344–5.

83. JAMES JOYCE, AD-WRITER. *transition*, Paris, 21 (Mar 1932) 258.

Rhymes written apropos of the London publication of *Anna Livia Plurabelle* and *Haveth Childers Everywhere*. Reprinted in Gorman, 1939, pp. 343–4.

84. EVELINE. *Golden Book*, New York, XVI.91 (Jul 1932) 58–61.

Reprinted from *Dubliners*. Other stories from *Dubliners* have been reprinted in the United States in *Good Literature*, Cleveland, *Lyric Love Stories*, New York, and *Encore*, New York.

85. FROM A BANNED WRITER TO A BANNED SINGER. *Hound & Horn*, New York, V.4 (Jul–Sept 1932) 542–6.

See also C 81.

86. ECCE PUER. *New Republic*, New York, LXXIII.939 (Nov 30, 1932) 70.

Included in *Collected Poems*, 1936 (A 44). Reprinted in the *Literary Digest*, New York, CXIV.25 (Dec 17, 1932) 46.

87. ECCE PUER. *Criterion*, London, XII.47 (Jan 1933) 184.

88. ECCE PUER. *Le Phare de Neuilly*, Neuilly-sur-Seine, 2 [Mar 1933] 25.

A photograph of the manuscript of the poem which is dated February 15, 1932, and a photograph of Joyce and his grandson. Accompanied by a French translation by Ivan Goll.

89. IL VENTO. *Sul Mare*, Trieste, IX.3 (May–June 1933) 45.

A translation into Italian by Joyce of the poem "Stephen's Green," by James Stephens.

90. FROM "WORK IN PROGRESS." *Contempo*, Chapel Hill, N.C., III.13 (Feb 15, 1934) 1.4 (FW 7–10).

91. THE MIME OF MICK, NICK AND THE MAGGIES. *Les Amis de 1914: Bulletin Hebdomadaire de l'Académie de la Coupole*, Paris, II.40 (Feb 23, 1934) 1 (FW 258–9).

92. COMMUNICATION DE M. JAMES JOYCE SUR LE DROIT MORAL DES ÉCRIVAINS. *XVe Congrès International de la Fédération P.E.N.*, Paris, June 1937, p. 24.
Not reprinted.

93. A PHOENIX PARK NOCTURNE. *Verve*, Paris, I.2 (Mar–June 1938) 26 (FW 244–6).

94. L'ESTHÉTIQUE DE JOYCE. *Études de Lettres*, Lausanne, XIII.1 (Oct 1, 1938) 39–40 (FW 244–6).
A reprint of "A Phoenix Park Nocturne" from *Verve*. It is analyzed in detail in an accompanying article by Jacques Mercanton. A footnote says that Mercanton was provided with many explanations by Joyce himself.

95. UNA LETTERA DI JOYCE. *Prospettive*, Rome, IV.4 (Apr 15, 1940) 11.
A letter to Ettore Settanni, cotranslator of *Anna Livia Plurabelle* into Italian, dated March 16, 1940, S. Gerand-Le-Puy. Not reprinted.

96. IL ROMANZACCIONE. *Prospettive*, Rome, IV.11–12 (Dec 15, 1940) 16.
A paragraph from a letter to Carlo Linati, dated Oct 10, 1920. Not reprinted.

97. THE JOYCE I KNEW. *Saturday Review of Literature*, New York, XXIII.14 (Jan 25, 1941) 16.
This article by Oliver St. John Gogarty includes Joyce's limerick on Lady Gregory and a two-line quotation from *The Holy Office*, quoted incorrectly.

98. JAMES JOYCE TO HIS LITERARY AGENTS. *More Books; the Bulletin of the Boston Public Library*, Boston, XVIII.1 (Jan 1943) 22.
Not reprinted.

99. JAMES JOYCE: A PORTRAIT OF THE ARTIST. *Tomorrow*, New York, VI.6 (Jan 1947) 23, 25–7.

This article by Oliver St. John Gogarty includes Joyce's limerick on Lady Gregory and a large portion of *Gas from a Burner* with a commentary by Gogarty.

100. CLAY. *Irish Digest*, Dublin, XXVIII.2 (Aug 1947) 91–6.
Reprinted from *Dubliners*.

101. IBSEN'S NEW DRAMA. *Contour*, Berkeley, Cal., 3 (Summer 1948) 49–60.
An unauthorized reprint of C 1.

102. CARTEGGIO INEDITO ITALO SVEVO—JAMES JOYCE. *Inventario*, Milan, II.1 (Spring 1949) 106–38.
This correspondence includes 6 letters from Joyce to Italo Svevo, 1921–28; 7 letters from Joyce to Livia Svevo, 1928–40; 4 letters from Italo Svevo to Joyce; and a preface by Harry Levin. English translation by Oreste Pucciani.

103. LILY MC CORMACK RECALLS. *Saturday Review of Literature*, New York, XXXII.44 (Oct 29, 1949) 51.
This article prints a paragraph from a letter from Joyce to John McCormack. Reprinted in *I Hear You Calling Me* (B 31).

104. JAMES JOYCE AS A FRIEND OF MUSIC. *Tomorrow*, New York, IX.4 (Dec 1949) 43.
This article by Oliver St. John Gogarty prints a parody by Joyce of Seumas O'Sullivan's poem "Praise."

105. THEY THINK THEY KNOW JOYCE. *Saturday Review of Literature*, New York, XXXIII.11 (Mar 18, 1950) 9.
This article by Oliver St. John Gogarty contains a reproduction of the first page of a letter from Joyce to Gogarty, June 3, 1904, the original of which is in the Manuscript Division, New York Public Library.

106. IL VENTO. *Irish Writing*, Cork, 11 (May 1950) 58.
A translation into Italian by Joyce of the poem "Stephen's Green," by James Stephens. A reprint of C 89.

107. LETTER TO ROBERT MC ALMON. *New York Times Book Review*, New York, LV.30 (Jul 23, 1950) 8.
An extract concerning Bernard Shaw's opinion of *Ulysses*. Also printed in *Time*, New York, LVI.6 (Aug 7, 1950) 33.

108. SOME UNPUBLISHED LETTERS OF JAMES JOYCE. *Envoy*, Dublin, v.17 (Apr 1951) 46–61.

Selected letters to his Aunt Josephine (Mrs. Murray), Harriet Shaw Weaver, Forrest Reid, Miss Guillermet, and Frank Budgen, dating from 1912 to 1930.

D. *Translations of Works by James Joyce*

BASIC ENGLISH

Periodicals:

1. THE ORTHOLOGICAL INSTITUTE. *Psyche*, London, 12.2 (Whole No. 46) (Oct 1931) 92–5.

A translation of the recorded portion of *Anna Livia Plurabelle* (FW 213–16) is incorporated in an article with the above title.

2. JAMES JOYCE'S ANNA LIVIA PLURABELLE IN BASIC ENGLISH. *transition*, Paris, 21 (Mar 1932) 259–62.

A reprint of the above translation.

CZECH

Books:

3. . . . DUBLIŇANÉ. Přeložil Josef Hrůša. Praha, Nakladatelství Jos. R. Vilímek, 1933. 304 pp. 17 x 12 cm. Kc. 32. Vilímkova Knihovna Svazek 310. 3,000 copies, in paper covers and in cloth. A translation of *Dubliners*.

4. . . . PORTRÉT MLADÉHO UMĚLCE. Praha, Václav Petr, 1930. 264 pp. 19.4 x 12.5 cm. 1,650 numbered copies, Nos. 1–50 on Holland van Gelder paper and Nos. 51–1650 on English Alfa paper. An authorized translation of *A Portrait of the Artist as a Young Man*, by Stasi Jilovske. Published with *Odysseus* (below) as a set, this work and the volumes of *Odysseus* being numbered together.

5. . . . ODYSSEUS (ULYSSES). Praha, Václav Petr, 1930. 3 vols. 19.1 x 12.8 cm. Translated by L. Vymětal. Published in an edition uniform with *Portrét Mladého Umělce* (above).

There is a copy of the edition of *Portrét Mladého Umělce* and *Odysseus* on Holland van Gelder paper in sheets enclosed in a green publisher's box in the Slocum Library.

6. Anna Livia PLURABELLA. Fragment Díla v zrodu (Work in Progress). Praha, Odeon, 1932. 98 pp. 18.5 x 12.5 cm. 300 numbered copies, Nos. 1–20 on Holland van Gelder paper and Nos. 21–300 on handmade paper. Translated by M. Weatherallová, Vladimír Procházka, and Adolf Hoffmeister.

DANISH

Books:

7\. . . . DUBLIN FORTÆLLINGER. Oversat af Ove Brusendorff. København, Athenæum, 1942. 232 pp. 19.8 x 13.2 cm. Kr. 7.50. A translation of *Dubliners*.

8\. . . . PORTRÆT AF KUNSTNEREN SOM UNGT MENNESKE. Oversat af Ove Brusendorff. København, Athenæum Dansk Forlag, 1941. 296 pp. 19.8 x 13.2 cm. Kr. 7.75. A translation of *A Portrait of the Artist as a Young Man*.

9\. . . . ULYSSES. Paa dansk ved Mogens Boisen. København, Martins Forlag, 1949. 768 pp. 19.8 x 12 cm. Kr. 24 (bound, Kr. 36). Published in November 1949 in paper covers, and also bound in three-quarters blue imitation leather; in slip case. Reprinted in December 1949.

ENGLISH

Periodical:

10\. CARTEGGIO INEDITO ITALO SVEVO—JAMES JOYCE. *Inventario*, Milan, II.1 (Spring 1949) 106–38.

A translation of Joyce's letters to Italo Svevo (Ettore Schmitz) from Triestine dialect into English by Oreste Pucciani. See C 102.

FINNISH

Book:

11\. . . . TAITEILIJAN OMAKUVA NUORUUDEN VUOSILTA, ROMAANI. Helsinki, Kustannusosakeyhtiö Tammi, [1946]. 324 pp. 20.2 x 14.5 cm.

A translation of *A Portrait of the Artist as a Young Man*, by Alex Matson.

FRENCH

Books:

12\. . . . POÈMES, avec des dessins en couleurs par A. Fornari. Paris, Les Chroniques du Jour, [1926]. [32] pp. 30.4 x 22.4 cm. Published

July 10, 1926, in an edition of 175 copies, 25 of which were *hors commerce.*

Includes *Chamber Music*, II, XI, XXIV, XV, translated by Auguste Morel, as well as poems by other writers. Two of these poems were reprinted in the periodical *Les Chroniques du Jour*, Paris, VII.6 (Nov 5, 1926). See D 26.

13. . . . GENS DE DUBLIN. Traduit de l'anglais par Yva Fernandez, Hélène du Pasquier, Jacques-Paul Reynaud. Préface de Valery Larbaud. Paris, Librairie Plon, Plon-Nourrit et Cie, 1926. 4 leaves, XXXVI, 320 pp., 2 leaves. 18.8 x 12 cm. Collection d'Auteurs Étrangers, publiée sous la direction de Charles Du Bos. 12 fr. Published April 15, 1926. Reprinted. A translation of *Dubliners.*

14. . . . GENS DE DUBLIN. Traduit de l'anglais. Lithographies de Charles Bardet. Lausanne, La Guilde du Livre, [1941]. 228 pp. Illus. 21.2 x 15.2 cm. La Guilde du Livre, Vol. XXXV. 4 Swiss fr. Published June 9, 1941, in an edition of 5,330 copies, including a special issue of 30 copies, *hors commerce*, for members of La Guilde du Livre. Omits "An Encounter," "Two Gallants," and "A Little Cloud."

15. DEDALUS; PORTRAIT DE L'ARTISTE JEUNE PAR LUI-MÊME. Roman . . . Traduit de l'anglais par Ludmila Savitzky. Paris, Éditions de la Sirène, [1924]. 280 pp. 23 x 15 cm. 10 fr. 75. Published March 22, 1924. Thirty-five special copies on handmade paper were also issued, of which Nos. 1–25 were sold and Nos. 26–35 were reserved for presentation. All copies have the initials *J.J.* in the colophon. This translation was republished October 27, 1943, by Gallimard, Paris, in an edition of 550 copies. A translation of *A Portrait of the Artist as a Young Man.*

16. . . . LES EXILÉS (EXILES) traduit de l'anglais par J. S. Bradley. trois actes. [Paris], nrf Gallimard, [1950]. 240 pp. 19 x 12 cm. Du Monde Entier XCII. 550 fr. Published in February 1950 in an edition of 1,255 copies, 205 of which were printed on Lafuma Navarre and 1,050 on alfa Marais, the latter being bound after the style of Paul Bonet. Reprinted, at 280 fr.

17. . . . ULYSSE. Traduit de l'anglais par M. Auguste Morel assisté par M. Stuart Gilbert. Traduction entièrement revue par M. Valery Larbaud avec la collaboration de l'auteur. Paris, La Maison des Amis

des Livres, Adrienne Monnier, 1929. [x], 874 pp. 23.3 x 18 cm. Published in February 1929, in an edition of 1,200 copies.

Statement of limitation: *Il a été tiré de cet ouvrage: 25 exemplaires sur Hollande Van Gelder, marqués* HOLLANDE VAN GELDER *et numérotés de 1 à 25. 100 exemplaires sur vélin d'Arches, marqués* VÉLIN D'ARCHES *et numérotés de 1 à 100. 875 exemplaires sur alfa vergé, marqués* ALFA VERGÉ *et numérotés de 1 à 875.*

Exemplaires d'auteur hors-commerce: 10 exemplaires sur Hollande Van Gelder, marqués EXEMPLAIRE D'AUTEUR *et marqués A à J. 20 exemplaires sur vélin d'Arches, marqués* EXEMPLAIRE D'AUTEUR *et numérotés de I à XX. 170 exemplaires sur alfa vergé, marqués* EXEMPLAIRE D'AUTEUR *et numérotés de 1 à 170.*

The copies on Hollande Van Gelder and vélin d'Arches measure 27.3 x 20.3 cm. and 24.4 x 19.3 cm., respectively.

A second printing of 3,500 copies of *Ulysse* was published by Adrienne Monnier and J.-O. Fourcade in January 1930. A third printing of 3,000 copies was published by La Maison des Amis des Livres in October 1930. This third printing was also issued by Gallimard, Paris, with a cancel title page and different covers.

In 1942 *Ulysse* was reissued by Gallimard in a binding after the style of Paul Bonet.

18. . . . STEPHEN LE HÉROS. Fragment de la première partie de Dedalus (Stephen Hero) traduit de l'anglais par Ludmila Savitsky. [Paris], nrf Gallimard, [1948]. 240 pp. 19.6 x 13.4 cm. 1050 fr. Published April 15, 1948, in an edition of 1,040 copies, in a binding after the style of Paul Bonet. The trade edition in paper covers was priced at 330 fr.

Periodicals:

19. ÉVELINE. *Les Écrits Nouveaux,* Paris, VIII.11 (Nov 1921) 31–6.

A translation of "Eveline" from *Dubliners,* by Mme Hélène du Pasquier.

20. L'ARABIE. *Les Écrits Nouveaux,* Paris, IX.2 (Fev 1922) 17–23.

A translation of "Araby" from *Dubliners,* by Mme Hélène du Pasquier.

21. UN INCIDENT RÉGRETTABLE. *La Revue de Genève,* Geneva, I.21 (Mars 1922) 359–69.

A translation of "A Painful Case" from *Dubliners,* by Yva Fernandez.

22. LES SOEURS. *Intentions*, Paris, I.5 (Mai 1922) 3–12.
A translation of "The Sisters" from *Dubliners* by Jacques-Paul Reynaud.

23. UN PETIT NUAGE. *Les Écrits Nouveaux*, Paris, IX.12 (Déc 1922) 3–16.
A translation of "A Little Cloud" from *Dubliners* by Yva Fernandez.

24. ULYSSE: FRAGMENTS. *Commerce*, Paris, I (Été 1924) 123–58.
A translation of *Ulysses* by Valery Larbaud and Auguste Morel (RH 4–17, 654–6, 663–4, 671, 682–3, 686, 688, 715–16, 721–2, 766–8).

25. ULYSSE (FRAGMENT). *900: Cahiers d'Italie et d'Europe*, Rome-Florence, I (Automne 1926) 107–31. Published September 21, 1926.
A translation of *Ulysses* by Auguste Morel (RH 54–69).

26. [Poèmes] *Les Chroniques du Jour*, Paris, VII.6 (Nov 5, 1926).
A translation of two poems from *Chamber Music* by Auguste Morel. See *Poèmes* [1926] listed with books (above).

27. CENDRES. *La Revue Nouvelle*, Paris, II.15 (Fév 15, 1926) 1–[7].
A translation of "Clay" from *Dubliners* by Yva Fernandez.

28. [Poèmes] *La Revue Nouvelle*, Paris, III.27 (Fév 15, 1927) 1–2.
A translation of *Chamber Music*, V and XXXVI, by Georges Duplaix.

29. ULYSSE (FRAGMENTS). *Les Feuilles Libres*, Paris, N.S. VIII.45–6 (Juin 1927) 173–6.
A translation of *Ulysses* by Valery Larbaud and Auguste Morel (RH 191, 337–9).

30. PROTÉE. *La Nouvelle Revue Française*, Paris, XV.179 (1 août 1928) [204]–226.
A translation of the third episode of *Ulysses* by Auguste Morel and Stuart Gilbert and reviewed by Valery Larbaud (RH 38–51). There were 12 offprints of this appearance.

31. POËMES D'API. *Bifur*, Paris, 3 (Sept 1929) 27–32.
Translations of "Tilly," "A Flower Given to My Daughter," "She Weeps Over Rahoon," "Tutto è Sciolto," "On the Beach at Fontana," "Simples," and "Alone," from *Pomes Penyeach*, by Auguste Morel.

32. ANNA LIVIA PLURABELLE. *La Nouvelle Revue Française*, Paris, XIX.212 (1 mai 1931) [633]–646.

A translation of *Finnegans Wake* (196–201, 215–16), by Samuel Beckett, Alfred Perron, Ivan Goll, Eugène Jolas, Paul L. Léon, Adrienne Monnier, and Philippe Soupault, with the author. There were two offprints of this appearance according to the La Hune Catalogue of Joyce's Paris Library.

33. ECCE PUER. *Le Phare de Neuilly*, Neuilly-sur-Seine, 2 [Mars 1933] between pp. 24 and 25.

A translation by Ivan Goll.

34. DE HONNI-SOIT A MAL-Y-CHANCE. *Mesures*, Paris, II.1 (Jan 15, 1936) 91–9.

A translation of *From a Banned Writer to a Banned Singer*, by Armand Petitjean, reviewed by the author. There were 8 numbered and signed offprints of this appearance.

35. POMES PENYEACH. *Fontaine*, Algiers, 37–40 (Numéro spécial 1944).

Translations of "A Flower Given to My Daughter," "Alone," "She Weeps Over Rahoon" and "Simples." No translators' names are given in this original appearance, but a subsequent book edition of this special number gives the initials J. M. R. and M.-P. F., the latter presumably the editor Max-Pol Fouchet.

36. LES ÉPIPHANIES: DEUX TEXTES INÉDITS DE JAMES JOYCE. *Arts*, Paris, 14 octobre 1949.

Translations of two of the "Epiphanies" listed in the La Hune Catalogue of Joyce's Paris Library, No. 159.

37. NOTES ET RÊVES. *84*, Paris, 12 (Nov 1949) 477–9.

Translations of three "Epiphanies." The first two are listed in the La Hune Catalogue as No. 159 (14 and 16); the third has not been identified. Translated by André du Bouchet.

38. LES EXILÉS. TROISIÈME ACTE. *L'Âge Nouveau*, Paris, 45 (Jan 1950) 3–23.

Translated by J. S. Bradley; introductory note and summary of Acts I and II by G.-A. Astre.

39. DANS LE SILLAGE DE FINNEGAN. *L'Âge Nouveau,* Paris, 45 (Jan 1950) 24–8.

A translation of *Finnegans Wake* (619, 624, 625–8, extracts only), by André du Bouchet. The English text is included.

40. POÈMES. *Mercure de France,* Paris, CCCIX.1041 (Mai-Août 1950) [5]–11.

Translations of *Chamber Music,* II, XI, XV, XXIV, XXXI, and "Tilly," "A Flower Given to My Daughter," "She Weeps Over Rahoon," "Tutto è Sciolto," "On the Beach at Fontana," "Simples," "Alone," and "Bahnhofstrasse," from *Pomes Penyeach,* by Annie Hervieu and Auguste Morel.

41. FINNEGANS WAKE FRAGMENT. *Roman,* Paris, 3 (Juin 1951) 270–1.

A translation of FW 627–8, by Maxime Chastaing and others.

GERMAN

Books:

42. . . . DUBLIN. NOVELLEN. Basel, etc., Rhein-Verlag, [1928]. 312 pp. 17.1 x 11.3 cm. M 3.25 (bound M 5). A translation of *Dubliners* by Georg Goyert. Printed in Switzerland. Reprinted.

The story "Eveline" in this translation was reprinted in *Die Fähre,* Munich, I.1 (1946) 5–9, and in *Silberboot Almanach,* Salzburg, (1946) 41–7.

43. . . . JUGENDBILDNIS. Basel, etc., Rhein-Verlag, [1926]. 374 pp., 1 leaf. 18.4 x 12 cm. M 5 (bound M 8). A translation of *A Portrait of the Artist as a Young Man,* by Georg Goyert. Printed in Switzerland. Listed in *Die Literarische Welt,* Berlin, II.16 (Apr 16, 1926) 8. Reprinted.

44. . . . VERBANNTE; Schauspiel in drei Akten. Zürich, Rascher & Cie, 1919. 154 pp., 1 leaf. 19.2 x 12.4 cm. 3.50 Swiss fr. A translation of *Exiles* by Hannah von Mettal. Published in March 1919 in an edition of 600 copies, at the expense of the author. An errata slip on pink paper is tipped in facing the title page.

An unascertained number of copies were apparently bound for the dramatic agents Oesterheld and Company, Berlin, and contain an additional title page with a notice on performance rights.

45. ULYSSES . . . Vom Verfasser geprüfte deutsche Ausgabe von Georg Goyert. [Basel], Privatdruck, 1927. 3 vols. 20 x 14 cm.

The first German edition of *Ulysses* appeared in four issues on laid paper and two on india paper. All but the first are in the Slocum Library.

1. An unspecified number of copies bound in full calf for the publisher. Covers with gold stamping on all edges. Limitation notice on recto of fourth preliminary leaf, Vol. I, with capital letter inserted in ink. The copy in the Joyce Paris Library inscribed to Joyce by Walther Lohmeyer, director of Rhein-Verlag, is copy "A," dated October 15, 1927.

2. An unspecified number of the 1,000 copies of this edition for sale bound in quarter brown leather with decorative paper sides over boards. Number printed in limitation notice. Copy examined was numbered "87."

3. Same as above but issued in green covers, presumably for purchasers who wished to have it bound for themselves. Imprint on front cover and spine reads: *Privatdruck 1927* . Copy examined was numbered "227."

4. Same as above but issued in blue covers. Imprint on front cover and spine reads: *Rhein-Verlag / Basel 1927* . At the bottom of the title page is printed: *Unnumeriertes Widmungsexemplar* . No limitation notice.

5. An unspecified number of the 100 press copies of this edition printed on india paper. Bound as three volumes in one, in red leather with green label containing author and title on spine. Base of spine reads: *Privatdruck für die Presse* . The limitation notice carries a lower-case letter inserted in ink. The copy examined was a presentation copy from Walther Lohmeyer to Ivan Goll, the Paris representative of Rhein-Verlag, and lettered "d." It was also inscribed by Joyce to Goll.

6. An unspecified number of the 100 press copies on india paper. Bound in blue cloth with a brown label containing author and title on spine. The number in the limitation notice is inserted in roman numerals in ink. Copy examined was numbered "LXXXXII."

The emphasis on the private nature of this publication and the strict limitation of copies was caused by some fear on the part of the Swiss publisher that *Ulysses* might be subject to censorship.

On February 10, 1927, Joyce wrote Claud Sykes to ask him if he would read proof for the German translation of *Ulysses*. The publication is listed in *Die Literarische Welt*, Berlin, III.44 (Oct 28, 1927) 8; the price, M 100.

Second and third German editions of *Ulysses* were published in 1930 by Rhein-Verlag, Zürich, in two volumes. The name of the publisher appears on the title pages of these editions.

46. Britanniens Neue Dichtung, an anthology, in German, of English modern verse by Yeats . . . James Joyce . . . and others, for the first time translated into German, by Karl Arns, with an introduction by Paul Selver. Münster, 1923. 8vo. Wrappers.

Not seen by the compilers. Title taken from *Rough Draft of the Catalogue of Books . . . in the Library of Edward W. Titus*, Cagnes-sur-Mer (A.M.), France, [n.d.], item No. 1224. This work was not listed in the sale catalogue of Mr. Titus, Parke-Bernet Galleries, N.Y., October 8–9, 1951.

47. EUROPÄISCHE LYRIK DER GEGENWART, 1900–1925. Josef Kalmer. Wien, Leipzig, Verlagsanstalt Zahn und Diamant, [1927]. 319 pp.

"Schauspieler im Spiegel um Mitternacht," p. 267. A translation of "A Memory of the Players in a Mirror at Midnight" from *Pomes Penyeach*, by Kalmer.

48. ENGLISCHE DICHTUNG, übertragen von Max Geilinger. Frauenfeld, [Switzerland], Huber, [1945]. 132 pp.

"Zwei Zürcher Gedichte: Allein [und] Bahnhofstrasse," by James Joyce, p. 125. These translations of "Alone" and "Bahnhofstrasse" from *Pomes Penyeach* were reprinted in *Atlantis*, Zürich, XX.6 (Juni 1948) 277.

49. . . . AUSGEWÄHLTE PROSA. Ausgewählt und eingeleitet von T. S. Eliot. . . . Zürich, Im Verlag der Arche, [1951]. 160 pp. 18.8 x 11.3 cm.

A translation of Eliot's *Introducing James Joyce*, 1942, using the translations of Georg Goyert. The selections from *Finnegans Wake* are not translated and a critical commentary by Carola Giedion-Welcker is substituted.

Also issued with the imprint of the Nymphenburger Verlagshandlung, Munich. Printed in Switzerland.

Periodicals:

50. EIN KAPITEL AUS JAMES JOYCE: "ULYSSES." *Die Literarische Welt*, Berlin, III.24 (June 17, 1927) [1]–2.

A translation of *Ulysses* (RH 101–3, 104, 105, 105–6, 106–8), by Georg Goyert.

51. DIE FÜNF WELTTEILE. Ein unidyllisches Verlegerjahrbuch. 1928. Basel, Rhein-Verlag, 1927.

Contains "Die Schwestern" ("The Sisters") from *Dubliners*, translated by Georg Goyert. Not seen by the compilers.

52. MITTERNÄCHTLICHE ERINNERUNG AN DIE KOMMÖDIANTEN VOR EINEM SPIEGEL. Aus "Pomes Penyeach," uebersetzt von Felix Béran. *Die Literarische Welt*, Berlin, VIII. 36/37 (Sept 2, 1932) 5.

A translation of "A Memory of the Players in a Mirror at Midnight."

53. Translations of "Alone" and "Bahnhofstrasse" from *Pomes Penyeach*, by Felix Béran, in the *Tages Anzeiger*, Zürich, in 1932 have not been seen by the compilers.

54. ALONE ALLEIN. *Die Fähre*, Munich, I.1 (1946) 9.

A translation of "Alone" from *Pomes Penyeach*, by Hermann Broch. This same translation appeared in *das silberboot*, Salzburg, II.1 (Mar 1946) 11.

55. ANNA LIVIA PLURABELLE. *Die Fähre*, Munich, I.6 (1946) 337–40.

A translation of *Finnegans Wake* (196–8, 213–15, 215–16), by Georg Goyert. This same translation appeared in *das silberboot*, Salzburg, II.8 (Oct or Nov 1946) 139–41.

GREEK

Periodicals:

56. O ODYSSEAS. *Kochlias*, Thessalonike, 1 (Dec 1945) 12–13.

A translation from *Ulysses* (RH 108–14), by Zoe Carelle, Giorges Kitsopoulos, Carolos Tzizek, Gianhes Svoronos, Nikos Gabriel Pentzikes, Leuteres Koniorlos, and Takes Iatrou.

57. O STEVEN PARA THIN' ALOS. *Kochlias*, Thessalonike, 6 (May 1946) 100–2.

A translation from *Ulysses* (RH 45–51), by Nikos Gabriel Pentzikes and Giorges Kitsopoulos.

HUNGARIAN

Book:

58. . . . ULYSSES. Fordította Gáspár Endre. [Budapest], Nova Irodalmi Intézet, [1947]. 2 vols. 24.2 x 16.8 cm.
This authorized translation was published in an edition of 1,000 copies.

ITALIAN

Books:

59. . . . MUSICA DA CAMERA. Venezia, Edizioni del Cavallino, 1943. 80 pp., 8 leaves containing 7 pictures of Joyce, 3 leaves. 24.7 x 16.2 cm. Translated by Marco Lombardi. Published in October 1943 in an edition of 990 copies. A translation of *Chamber Music.*

60. GENTE DI DUBLINO. Racconti . . . Milano, Edizioni Corbaccio, [1933]. 336 pp. 17.9 x 11.1 cm. L. 5. I Corvi; Collana Universale Moderna, Numero 11. Translated by Annie and Adriano Lami. Published in March 1933. A translation of *Dubliners.*

61. Gente di Dublino . . . [Torino], Einaudi, 1949. 272 pp., 2 leaves. 19.5 x 12.8 cm. L. 600 (in cloth, L. 700). I Coralli 35. Translated by Franca Cancogni. Published on March 9, 1949.

62. . . . ARABY. Versione dall' Inglese di Amalia Risolo. Trieste, Casa Editrice Triestina Carlo Moscheni, [1935]. 154 pp., 1 leaf. 20.2 x 14.7 cm. Contents: *James Joyce* (*Biografia essenziale*) [dated October 29, 1934]—*Araby—Una nuvoletta* ["A Little Cloud"]—*Controparti* ["Counterparts"]—*Evelina—I morti* ["The Dead"]. These five stories were selected from *Dubliners.*

63. . . . DEDALUS; RITRATTO DELL'ARTISTA DA GIOVANE. Prefazione di Alberto Rossi; Versione di Cesare Pavese. Torino, Frassinelli Tipografo-Editore, 1933. xxvi, 1 leaf, 378 pp., 1 leaf. 18.4 x 12.7 cm. L. 15. Biblioteca Europea, diretta da Franco Antonicelli v. The preface is dated May 1933. A translation of *A Portrait of the Artist as a Young Man.*

A revised second edition was published on April 30, 1942; a third edition on July 20, 1943.

64. . . . ESULI (1918). Milano, Rosa e Ballo Editori, 1944. XII, 150 pp., port. 15.8 x 11.9 cm. Collana Teatro Moderno, a Cura di Paolo Grassi [1]. Translated by Carlo Linati. Published in July 1944. A translation of *Exiles*.

This volume also contains a photograph of Joyce with a facsimile inscription to Carlo Linati, p. [6]; a letter from Joyce to Carlo Linati, Trieste, December 10, 1919, pp. ix–x; and a brief note on Joyce and his work, pp. 145–6. See B 25.

65. . . . POESIE DA UN SOLDO; DALL' "ULISSE." Milano, Enrico Cederna, [1949]. 116 pp., 4 leaves. 20.4 x 13 cm. Edited and presumably translated by Alberto Rossi. Published in June 1949 in an edition of 2,000 copies, of which 100 were not for sale. A translation of *Pomes Penyeach* and the third (Proteus) episode of *Ulysses* (RH 38–51). The English text is included on facing pages, and there are facing title pages in English and in Italian.

This volume also contains "James Joyce e la Poesia," by Alberto Rossi, pp. 9–[26]

66. . . . STEFANO EROE. Con otto illustrazioni di Luigi Broggini. [Milano], Arnoldo Mondadori Editore, [1950]. 302 pp., 3 leaves. 20.3 x 13.8 cm. L. 1800. Il Ponte, I Grandi Narratori Italiani e Stranieri XXVI. Translated by Carlo Linati. Published in December 1950. A translation of *Stephen Hero*.

Includes the introduction by Theodore Spencer, translated by Giorgio Monicelli.

Periodicals:

67. ESULI. *Il Convegno*, Milan, I.3 (Apr 1920) 27–52.
A translation of Act I of *Exiles*, by Carlo Linati.

68. ESULI. *Il Convegno*, Milan, I.4 (May 1920) 27–46.
A translation of Act II of *Exiles*, by Carlo Linati.

69. ESULI. *Il Convegno*, Milan, I.5 (June 1920) 22–37.
A translation of Act III of *Exiles*, by Carlo Linati.

70. ARABY. *Il Convegno*, Milan, V.5 (May 1924) 301–8.
A translation of "Araby" from *Dubliners*, by Carlo Linati.

71. DA L' "ULYSSES" DI JAMES JOYCE. *Il Convegno*, Milan, VII.11–12 (Nov–Dec 1926) 813–28.

A translation from *Ulysses*, by Carlo Linati.

72. UN CASO PENOSO, RACCONTO DI JAMES JOYCE. *La Fiera Letteraria*, Milan, IV.23 (June 3, 1928) 5.

A translation of "A Painful Case" from *Dubliners*, by Giacomo Prampolini. Illustrated by M. Vellani-Marchi.

73. UN CASO PIETOSO. *Il Convegno*, Milan, X.5 (May 1929) 258–67.

A translation of "A Painful Case" from *Dubliners* by Nina Ruffini.

74. ULISSE I° EPISODIO. *Il Convegno*, Milan, XII.9–10 (Oct 1931) 476–502.

A translation from *Ulysses* (RH 4–24), by Alberto Rossi.

75. TRE POESIE DI JAMES JOYCE. *Circoli*, Genoa, II.1 (Jan–Feb 1932) 35–41.

Translations of *Chamber Music*, XXXV and XXXVI, and "On the Beach at Fontana" from *Pomes Penyeach*, by Glauco Natoli. English text also included.

76. *Il Mattino*, Naples. Sometime prior to February 13, 1932, a translation of a work by Joyce appeared in this Neapolitan newspaper. It has not been identified.

77. ODO UN ESERCITO. *Occidente*, Rome, II.5 (Oct–Dec 1933) 80.

A translation of "I Hear an Army," *Chamber Music*, XXXVI, by Aldo Philipson.

78. ANNA LIVIA PLURABELLA. *Prospettive*, Rome, IV.2 (Feb 15, 1940) 13–15.

A translation of *Finnegans Wake* (196), by James Joyce and Ettore Settanni. According to the La Hune Catalogue of Joyce's Paris Library, No. 344, this and the following item were really the work of Joyce and Nino Frank. Settanni appropriated the work of Frank during the war.

79. I FIUMI SCORRONO. *Prospettive*, Rome, IV. 11–12 (Dec 15, 1940) 14–16.

A translation of *Finnegans Wake* (215–16), by James Joyce and Ettore Settanni.

80. LA TEORIA DELLA EPIFANIE. *Inventario*, Florence, I.2 (Summer 1946) 54–6.

A translation from *Stephen Hero* (New Directions edition 210–13), by Luigi Berti.

JAPANESE

Books:

81. SHITSU GAKU. Translated by Chika Sagawa. Tokyo, Shinoki Sha, 1933.

A translation of *Chamber Music*.

82. DABURIN NO HITO BITO. Translated by Tei Nagamatsu. Tokyo, Kinsei Do, 1931. 350 pp., 1 leaf. 18.4 x 12.5 cm.

A translation of *Dubliners*.

83. DABURIN SHISEIJI. Translated by Ichiro Ando. Tokyo, Kobundo Shobo, 1940–41. 2 vols. 17.5 x 10.5 cm.

A translation of *Dubliners*.

Reprinted in 1952 by Kawaide Shobo.

84. THE DEAD . . . Introduction by Arundell del Re. Translated by I. Ando. Tokyo, Kaitakusha, 1930. 3 leaves, 220 pp., 1 leaf. Port. 16.8 x 11 cm. The Modern English Literature Series.

From *Dubliners*. The English text and notes are included. The paper wrappers are an imitation of those of the volumes published by the Modern Library, New York.

85. EI BEI TAN-PEN-SHU (English and American Short Stories). Translated by Tomoji Abe. Tokyo, Kawaide Shobo, 1926. 425 pp.

Includes "A Painful Case" from *Dubliners*.

86. TAN-PEN-SHU (Short Stories). Translated by Tei Nagamatsu. Tokyo, Kinsei Do, 1932. 3 leaves, 80 pp., 2 leaves. 19.1 x 13.7 cm.

Consists of "A Little Cloud," "Araby," "Eveline," "Clay," and "Two Gallants" from *Dubliners*.

87. WAKAKI HI NO GEIJUTSUKA NO JIGAZO. Translated by Matsuji Ono and Tomio Yokobori. Tokyo, Sogensha, 1932. 4 leaves, 454 pp., 6 leaves. 19.5 x 14 cm.

A translation of *A Portrait of the Artist as a Young Man*.

88. WAKAKI HI NO GEIJUTSUKA JIGAZO. Translated by Kozaburo Nabara. Tokyo, Iwanami, 1937. 441, 19 pp. 15.8 x 10.3 cm.

A translation of *A Portrait of the Artist as a Young Man.*

89. IPPEN SHI SHU. Translated by Chiaki Kitamura. Tokyo, Shinoki Sha, 1933.

A translation of *Pomes Penyeach.*

90. JOISU SHISHU. Translated by Junzaburo Nishiwaki. Tokyo, Dai Ichi Shobo, 1933.

Translations from *Chamber Music*, *Pomes Penyeach*, and *Anna Livia Plurabelle.*

91. ULYSSES. Translated by Tadashi Ito, Sadamu Nagamatsu, and Hisanori Tsujino. Tokyo, Dai Ichi Shobo, 1931–34. 2 vols.

Vol. II of this edition is usually found with pp. 516–97 cut out, presumably because of censorship. These pages are omitted from the second and later printings.

92. ULYSSES. Translated by Sohei Morita, Hirosaburo Nahara, Naotaro Tatsuguchi, Kenji Ono, Ichiro Ando, Eitaro Murayama. Tokyo, Iwanami Shoten, 1932–35. 5 vols.

93. ULYSSES. Translated by Sei Ito. Tokyo, Kawaide Shobo, [n.d.]. 208 pp. Not a complete translation.

Periodicals:

The compilers have a record (usually incomplete) of approximately thirty periodical appearances of works by Joyce translated into Japanese, as well as many articles in Japanese concerning Joyce and his work. They hope to publish this list of periodical translations and articles at some future time.

NORWEGIAN

Book:

94. . . . Portrett av kunstneren som ung mann. Oversatt av Niels Chr. Brøgger. Oslo, Ernst G. Mortensens Forlag, 1948. 310 pp., 1 blank leaf. 19.8 x 13.1 cm.

A translation of *A Portrait of the Artist as a Young Man.*

POLISH

See F 31 for Polish translations of four poems from *Chamber Music.*

Book:

95. . . . PORTRET ARTYSTY Z CZASÓW MŁODOŚCI. Z upoważnienia autora przełożył Zygmunt Allan. Warszawa, Towarzystwo Wydawnicze "Rój," 1931. 328 pp. 19.2 x 12.5 cm.

A translation of *A Portrait of the Artist as a Young Man.*

PORTUGUESE

Books:

96. . . . OS MELHORES CONTOS DE JAMES JOYCE. Lisboa, Editorial Hélio, 1946. 228 pp. Colecção "Antologia" 3. Selected and translated by María da Paz Ferreira.

Contains 10 stories from *Dubliners* and an essay, "James Joyce e a Sua Obra," by João Gaspar Simões.

97. . . . CONTOS INGLÊSES MODERNOS . . . Selecção e prefácio de Carmo Vaz. Lisboa, Editorial "Gleba," [n.d.]. 264 pp. Colecção "Contos e Novelas" 21.

Contains "O Morto" ["The Dead"] from *Dubliners,* translated by Carmo Vaz, pp. 35–90.

98. OS MELHORES CONTOS INGLÊSES. Primeira Série. Traduzidos do inglês por Cabral do Nascimento. Selecção e prefácio de João Gaspar Simões. Lisboa, Portugália Editora, [n.d.]. 440 pp. Antologias Universais Conto III.

Contains "Arábia" ["Araby"] from *Dubliners,* pp. 215–25.

99. . . . RETRATO DO ARTISTA QUANDO JOVEM. Tradução de José Geraldo Vieira. Pôrto Alegre, [Brazil], Edição da Livraria do Globo, [1945]. 250 pp., 1 leaf. Port. 19.3 x 14 cm. Coleção Nobel, Vol. 61.

A translation of *A Portrait of the Artist as a Young Man.*

RUSSIAN

Books:

100. DUBLINTZY (Dubliners). Rasskazy. Perevod s angliĭskovo E. N. Fedotovoĭ. Leningrad, Izdatelstvo "Mysl," 1927. 168 pp. 17.5 x 13 cm. 1 ruble. Paper covers.

Contains "Araby," "Eveline," "After the Race," "Two Gallants," "The Boarding House," "A Little Cloud," "Counterparts," "Clay," "A

Painful Case," "Ivy Day in the Committee Room," and "The Dead," with a foreword by the translator.

There is a copy of this work in the Slavonic Division, New York Public Library.

101. DUBLINTZY. Roman, pereviol s angliĭskovo pod redaktziyeĭ I. A. Kashkina. Moscow, Goslitizdat, 1937.

Not seen by the compilers. Listed in *Knizhnaya letopis'*, No. 59, No. 35626 (1937).

Periodicals:

All entries except the first are from *Letopis' zhurnal'nykh stateĭ*, Moscow, 1926–.

102. [Passages from] ULYSSES. *Novinki zapada*, Moscow, 1925. Listed in *Bol'shaya sovetskaya entziklopediya*, Vol. 21 (1931) columns 802–3.

103. UTRO M-RA BLUMA. Translated by Val. Stenich. *Literaturnĭ sovremennik*, Leningrad, 5 (1935) 131–59. A translation of "The morning of Mr. Bloom," from *Ulysses*, with a foreword by D. S. Mirsky.

104. ULYSSES. Translations of portions of *Ulysses* by various hands appeared in the following numbers of the Russian-language edition of *International Literature* (*Internatzional'naya literatura*, Moscow): 1 (1935) 61–73; 2 (1935) 43–50; 3 (1935) 55–66; 4 (1935) 106; 9 (1935) 43–52; 10 (1935) 85–95; 11 (1935) 54–62; 12 (1935) 45–55; 1 (1936) 51–70; 2 (1936) 52–73; 3 (1936) 53–76; 4 (1936) 66–8, 69–91; 1 (1937) 196–202; 12 (1939) 203–9; 1 (1940) 185–8.

105. PRISKORBNYĬ SLUCHAĬ. Translated by N. Daruzes. *30 dneĭ*, Moscow, XII.9 (1936) 47–54. A translation of "A Painful Case," from *Dubliners*. Illustrated.

106. MAT'. Translated by N. Daruzes. *30 dneĭ*, Moscow, XII.11 (1936) 57–64. A translation of "A Mother" from *Dubliners*. Illustrated.

SPANISH

Books:

107. . . . DUBLINESES (DUBLINERS). Traducción de L. A. Sanchez. Santiago, Chile, Ediciones Ercilla, 1945 [*c*. 1941]. 196 pp. 21.9 x 14 cm.

Omits "A Mother" and "Grace."

108. LOS MUERTOS. Barcelona, Editorial Grano de Oro, 1941. 147 pp. 19 x 16 cm.

A translation of "The Dead" from *Dubliners*.

109. GENTE DE DUBLIN . . . Traducción de I. Abelló. Barcelona, Editorial Tartessos, [1942]. 248 pp. 17.1 x 10 cm. 17 ptas. Narradores contemporaneos 1. Published in September 1942, under the direction of Felix Ros. A translation of *Dubliners*.

110. EL ARTISTA ADOLESCENTE (RETRATO) . . . Traducido del inglés por Alfonso Donado. Prólogo de Antonio Marichalar. Madrid, Biblioteca Nueva, 1926. 338 pp., 1 blank leaf. Illus. 19.2 x 12.5 cm. 5 ptas.

A translation of *A Portrait of the Artist as a Young Man.*

111. . . . EL ARTISTA ADOLESCENTE. Traducción directa del inglés por Alfonso Donado. Prólogo de Hugo Galasso Vicari. Santiago, Chile, Editorial Osiris, [1935]. 252 pp., 4 pages of advertisements. 19.5 x 13.5 cm. 6 pesos. Coleccion Osiris No. 74.

112. . . . EL ARTISTA ADOLESCENTE (RETRATO). Buenos Aires, etc., Espasa-Calpe Argentina, S.A., [1938]. 294 pp., 1 leaf. 17.9 x 11.3 cm. $2.25 (pesos). Coleccion Austral [29]. Translated by Alfonso Donado. Published February 5, 1938.

113. . . . EL ARTISTA ADOLESCENTE (RETRATO). Traducido del inglés por Alfonso Donado. Prólogo de Antonio Marichalar. Caratula de Horna. Mexico, D.F., Editorial Ur, [n.d.].

114. . . . DESTERRADOS ("EXILES") COMEDIA EN TRES ACTOS. Buenos Aires, Sur, [1937]. 238 pp., 1 leaf. 18.5 x 13.5 cm. $2.25 (pesos). Translated under the direction of A. Jiménez Fraud. Published October 11, 1937.

115. . . . ULISES. Traducido por J. Salas Subirat. Buenos Aires, Santiago Rueda, ed., [1945]. XVI, 834 pp., 3 leaves. 22.3 x 14.2 cm. Published under the direction of Max Dickmann. This translation of *Ulysses* was prepared during the years 1940–45.

Colophon: *"Ulises" se terminó de imprimir bajo el sello editorial de Santiago Rueda el 14 de Julio de 1945, en Artes Gráficas Bartolomé u. Chiesino que cuidó la parte artística. El tiraje está limitado a 28 ejemplares en dos volúmenes en papel Liverpool Ledger señalados de A a Z. 300 ejemplares en dos volúmenes en papel Especial numerados de 1 a 300. 2200 ejemplares en un volumen en papel Polar, que constituyen la edición original encuadernada por la casa Botto.*

Reprinted January 15, 1949, by Editorial Diana, Mexico, D.F., in an edition of 5,000 copies.

Periodicals:

116. LA ULTIMA HOJA DEL ULISES. *Proa*, Buenos Aires, II.6 (Jan 1925) 8–9.

A translation from *Ulysses* (RH 766–8), by Jorge Luis Borges.

117. DOS ENTRETENIDOS. *Hoy*, Santiago, Chile, IV.197 (Aug 30, 1935) 50–3.

A translation of a portion of "Two Gallants" from *Dubliners.*

118. EVELINE. *Hoy*, Santiago, Chile, IV.200 (Sept 17, 1935) 67–9.

A translation of a portion of "Eveline" from *Dubliners.*

119. LA CASA DE PENSION. *Hoy*, Santiago, Chile, VI.286 (May 13, 1937) 76–8.

A translation of a portion of "The Boarding House" from *Dubliners.*

120. UNA ESCENA DE DESTERRADOS. *Sur*, Buenos Aires, VII (Aug 1937) 68–86.

A translation of a portion of the second act of *Exiles*, by A. Jiménez Fraud.

SWEDISH

Books:

121. DUBLIN-NOVELLER . . . Från Engelskan av Emilie Kullman. Stockholm, Wahlström & Widstrand, [1931]. 216 pp. 19.4 x 12.6 cm. Kr. 4.75.

A translation of *Dubliners*, omitting "Ivy Day in the Committee Room."

122. ETT PORTRÄTT AV FÖRFATTAREN SOM UNG . . . Bemynd.Översättning av Ebba Atterbom . . . Stockholm, Hugo Gebers Förlag, [1921]. 2 leaves, 272 pp. 19.5 x 12.7 cm. Kr. 7.50.

A translation of *A Portrait of the Artist as a Young Man.*

123. . . . Odysseus. Stockholm, Albert Bonniers Förlag, [1946]. 772 pp. 19.4 x 11.9 cm. Kr. 15 (bound, Kr. 18.50). Panache Serien. A translation of *Ulysses*, by Thomas Warburton. Issued in wrappers and in three-quarters cloth.

URDU

Periodicals:

124. TA C-AME KHANE. *Afsaneh*, Lahore, India, 1.1 (Apr 3, 1933) 9–15.
A translation of a portion of "The Boarding House" from *Dubliners*.

E. *Manuscripts of James Joyce*

THIS SECTION is divided into two parts: manuscripts of principal works; and manuscripts of other writings (including periodical material and material contributed to books), as well as unpublished manuscript material not mentioned in books. Uniform descriptions have not been attempted because in many cases it has been impossible to examine the manuscripts in detail. The exact location of manuscripts (when known) is usually given only for public institutions and the Slocum Library.

MANUSCRIPTS OF PRINCIPAL WORKS

1. *Chamber Music* (1907).

No original manuscript of *Chamber Music, per se*, is known to exist. The following, with the possible exception of *e.i*, *e.ii*, and *e.iii*, were written out by Joyce after the actual composition of the poems.

a. Manuscript described in the catalogue issued by Sylvia Beach, Shakespeare and Company, Paris, May 15, 1935, item No. 8, as follows: "The original manuscript of 33 of the 36 poems that compose this work. 27 are written on large sheets, 17 x 11½ ins., of handsome laid paper with a watermark representing a shamrock and a sun, etc., and 6 on inferior paper, 13 x 8 ins. It was from this manuscript, specially prepared for the occasion, that in 1902 the youthful James Joyce read aloud his poems to W. B. Yeats."

It is unlikely that this is the "original" manuscript, but on the basis of textual comparisons it certainly precedes the following. It contains the first 34 poems of *Chamber Music*, with the exception of No. XXI.

This manuscript was sold for Miss Beach by Marian Willard to a New York collector. It was offered for sale by several dealers in 1947 and is now privately owned in New York.

b. Manuscript of the first 34 poems of *Chamber Music* written on inferior copy paper, similar to that used for the stories of *Dubliners* (see below). 21 x 17 cm. The text is written on the recto of 34 leaves, followed by a blank leaf and preceded by two leaves, the first of which bears the notation "MS" and the second, the title "*Chamber Music*, (a suite of thirty-four songs for lovers) by James Joyce." It also bears the address "Via S. Nicolò, 30,ii° Trieste, Austria," and the date "1905."

This manuscript was given by Joyce to his brother Stanislaus, who in turn gave it to the art critic Bernard Berenson. Berenson gave it back to Stanislaus Joyce several years later. It is now in the Slocum Library.

In both manuscripts *a* and *b* the order of the poems is quite different from that of the final edition, and only with the second manuscript does the title *Chamber Music* appear. In spite of Oliver St. John Gogarty's claim that he was present at an incident that resulted in the naming of the book (see his *Mourning Became Mrs. Spendlove,* New York, Creative Age Press, 1948, p. 55), this fact would bear out Stanislaus Joyce's statement that he both gave the collection its title and was responsible for the final arrangement.

Of this version at least two copies must have existed, and possibly three. Arthur Symons sent one to Grant Richards in September 1904. What happened to this is unknown, but Joyce sent him another copy on August 17, 1905, and on October 15, 1905, he made still another copy and sent it to Constable. On October 17, 1906, Joyce wrote Elkin Mathews that he was rearranging the manuscript and would send it in a few days. This is undoubtedly the next item *c* in this list. Grant Richards returned one manuscript to Joyce just prior to December 2, 1907.

c. Final manuscript from which the Elkin Mathews edition of 1907 was set. On inferior copy paper as above, approximately 17 x 21 cm. Thirty-six leaves, preceded by a title page, in stiff blue paper wrappers, all held together by a copper pin. The title page, which is possibly not in Joyce's hand, reads: "*Chamber Music* by James Joyce Ms. 24 October 1906: Rome." The last page is signed at the bottom lower right: "Jas A Joyce 24 October 1906 Via Frattina 52.II.Rome." Contains printer's instructions in pencil. This manuscript was secured from a private owner by the Slocum Library.

d. Manuscript copied by Joyce on vellum from the printed version and presented to his wife, Christmas 1909. It is described in the La Hune Catalogue, 1949, No. 65, as follows:

Un fort cahier 18 x 23.5 cm. de 40 pages de parchemin montées sur onglet. Relié plein chagrin beige orné de bandes transversales en chagrin rouge, grain long, serties de filets d'or. Entre les bandes du premier plat monogramme N. J. en mosaïque rouge traversé d'un bandeau sur pointillé d'or "1909". Entre les bandes du second plat armoiries de la famille Joyce en mosaïque noire et rouge pour l'écu, grise pour les ornements extérieurs.

The description continues to say that at the beginning Joyce has written the dedication: "To my darling Nora Christmas 1909." On a subsequent page Joyce has also written: "This copy of my poems was made by me in Dublin and finished on the eleventh of November of the year 1909." This manuscript copy is now in the Lockwood Memorial Library, University of Buffalo.

e. Miscellaneous manuscripts of *Chamber Music.*

i. Nos. I, V, XXIV, XXVIII, and XXXIV, and a sixth unpublished poem of three quatrains beginning:

> Come out to where the youth is met
> Under the moon, beside the sea.

A note with these poems says: "Evidently first drafts, written on separate scraps of ruled paper torn from copy books. Each is entirely in Joyce's hand and signed with his initials [J. A. J.]" The text of these poems is that of the printed version and they may have been considered final drafts.

ii. A post card to J. Francis Byrne, December 15, 1902, from the Hotel Corneille, Paris, with the title: "Second Part—Opening which tells of the journeying of the soul." The text is No. XXXV of *Chamber Music*. This post card is now in the Slocum Library.

iii. Constantine P. Curran of Dublin has two or three manuscript poems of *Chamber Music,* presented to him by Joyce in 1903 or 1904.

iv. A portion of a single poem copied by Joyce into the autograph album of a woman now living in Brooklyn, New York.

2. *Dubliners* (1914).

No complete manuscript of *Dubliners* is known.

a. "The Sisters," written on the recto of 10 numbered leaves, 21 x 17 cm. Acquired from a private owner by the Slocum Library.

b. "An Encounter," written on the recto of 16 leaves, 21 x 17 cm. The first leaf bears the title "An Encounter" and is followed by the text of 14 numbered leaves; the last leaf is blank. With printer's instructions. Acquired from a private owner by the Slocum Library.

c. "The Boarding House," written on the recto of 17 numbered leaves, 21 x 17 cm. Signed on the last leaf: "Stephen Daedalus, via San Nicolò 30 ii° 1.7.05." Acquired from a private owner by the Slocum Library.

d. "Counterparts," written on the recto of 24 numbered leaves, 21 x 17 cm. Last leaf missing. Acquired from a private owner by the Slocum Library.

e.i. "A Painful Case," written on the recto of 20 numbered leaves, 21 x 17 cm. Last leaf missing. Possibly the original manuscript since there are many corrections both in the margins and in the body of the text, which differs from the final version. Acquired from a private owner by the Slocum Library.

ii. "A Painful Case," written on the recto of 24 leaves, 21 x 17 cm. The first leaf bears the title "A Painful Case" and is followed by the text of 22 numbered leaves. Leaf 22 is signed *JAJ 15.8.05* . Last leaf blank. This manuscript was given by Joyce to Sylvia Beach who described it in her catalogue of 1935. It was purchased by C. A. Stonehill of London and New Haven, Connecticut, who sold it to the Scribner Book Store, from whom it was acquired by the Slocum Library.

f. "Ivy Day in the Committee Room," written on the recto of 23 numbered leaves, 21 x 17 cm. Signed on the last leaf *Jas A Joyce 29 August 1905* . Acquired from a private owner by the Slocum Library.

g. "A Mother," written on the recto of 18 leaves, 21 x 17 cm. The first leaf bears the title *A Mother* and is followed by the text of 16 numbered leaves. Last leaf blank. Acquired from a private owner by the Slocum Library.

h. "Grace," written on the recto of 36 leaves, 21 x 17 cm. The first leaf bears the title *Grace* and is followed by the text of 34 numbered leaves. Last leaf blank. Provenance same as *e.ii*, above.

i. "The Dead," written on the recto of 20 leaves, 21 x 17 cm. Numbered 1–16, 74–7. Provenance same as *e.ii*, above. Subsequently the first leaf with the title *The Dead* and leaves 17–19 and 57 were acquired from a private owner by the Slocum Library.

Of the 10 manuscripts of stories described above, all but "The Boarding House," "Counterparts," the incomplete version of "A Painful Case" (*e.i*), and "Ivy Day in the Committee Room" contain printer's instructions.

j. Manuscript of corrections to *Dubliners* (1914). One leaf, 33.6 x 21 cm. Of the 30 corrections contained on this leaf, only 7 were ever made in any subsequent editions. These were made not from this leaf but on the judgment of proofreaders. This manuscript of corrections was sent by Joyce to Grant Richards on February 2, 1915, in anticipation of a second English edition of *Dubliners*. In March 1917 Joyce wrote Richards to ask whether these corrections had been forwarded to Huebsch. Early in June Mrs. Joyce wrote J. B. Pinker, Joyce's agent, asking that the *Dubliners* corrections, along with those for the *Portrait*, be sent to "his American publishers" and that "These MSS are to be given to Mr. John Quinn." A month later Joyce wrote Quinn saying that he saw that he had the corrections. This leaf was bought by the Brick Row Book Shop, New York, at the sale of John Quinn's Library, Anderson Galleries, New York, November 1923–March 1924, item No. 4921. The Brick Row Book Shop sold it to H. Bacon Collamore of Hartford, Connecticut, who in turn sold it to the Scribner Book Store in 1948, from whom it was acquired by the Slocum Library.

3. *A Portrait of the Artist as a Young Man* (1916).

a. Manuscript described by Sylvia Beach in her catalogue of 1935, No. 10, as follows:

Holograph manuscript in a copybook 8 1/2 x 6 3/4 ins., 20 close-written pages. Signed Jas. A. Joyce with date: 7/1/1904. On inside of back cover the Author has written the following explanation: *Note.—These preceding pages are the first draft of* A PORTRAIT OF THE ARTIST AS A YOUNG MAN *and a sketch of the plot and characters written (January 1904) in a copybook of my sister Mabel (b 1896, d 1911). The essay was written for a Dublin review* DANA *but refused insertion by the editors Mr. W. K. Magee (John Eglington* [sic]) *and Mr. Frederick Ryan.* Signed 'James Joyce' and the date.

This copybook is still in the possession of Miss Beach.

b.i. Manuscript described by Sylvia Beach in her catalogue of 1935, No. 9, as follows: "Holograph manuscript of the FIRST VERSION of this work; incomplete, 370 pages, numbered 519 to 902, closely but legibly written, in ink on sheets 21 x 17 ins., with marks in red pencil. This first version of 'A Portrait of the Artist as a Young Man,' which dates from 1903, is quite unlike the present version of James Joyce's novel."

This manuscript was purchased from Miss Beach by Theodore Spencer for Harvard University in 1938 or 1939, funds for the purchase being raised by subscription. It was edited with a preface by Spencer and published in 1944 with the title *Stephen Hero*. At the time this manuscript was offered for sale, April 7, 1934, Joyce wrote

Harriet Shaw Weaver: "Honestly, however, I dislike the putting up for sale of the first MS of the *Portrait*, about 1000 pages. And what rubbish it is!"

ii. Twenty-five additional pages of *b.i*, 21 x 17 cm., numbered 477–8, 481–9, 491–7, 499–505. Acquired from a private owner by the Slocum Library.

The first page begins with the last part of the diary entry of April 16 in *A Portrait* (H 299). A gap follows across which is written *Departure for Paris* in blue crayon. The rest of the manuscript concerns a visit by Stephen Dedalus to his godfather "Mr. Fulham" in Mullingar some time after he had started at University College. (Joyce visited Mullingar in the summers of both 1900 and 1901.)

c. The final manuscript, given by Joyce to Harriet Shaw Weaver. Of this work Miss Weaver wrote to the compilers on February 29, 1952:

The final manuscript of *A Portrait of the Artist* (fair copy in ink written in very clear handwriting and with no corrections) was sent to me in 1920 from Trieste by Mr Joyce and was given by me in July 1951 to the National Library of Ireland, Dublin. From the typescript, made in Trieste, of the manuscript and sent—the first three chapters to Mr Pound, the last two, later, to me—*The Egoist* serial was set up and, except for corrections of printers' errors and their ideas as to punctuation which were not Mr Joyce's! practically no other alterations were made for the printing of the book itself.

d. Manuscript of corrections to be made to the first edition of *A Portrait* (1916). Seven numbered leaves, 36 x 22.5 cm. These 364 corrections were made in all English and Continental editions after the first Egoist edition (excluding the third Egoist edition which was published with American sheets). The greater part of these corrections were never made in American printings and there is some doubt whether or not B. W. Huebsch ever saw them. Those corrections that were made were at the instance of proofreaders. In March 1917 Joyce wrote J. B. Pinker, his agent, that "The novel does not seem to have been read." He said that he was sending corrections for forwarding to New York. On April 10 he sent Pinker the corrections and asked that they be typed and forwarded to Huebsch. From that time their history has been the same as that of the single leaf of *Dubliners* corrections (E 2.*j*).

Sylvia Beach in her catalogue of 1935 states that Joyce threw the manuscript of *Stephen Hero* into the fire on its twentieth rejection and that it was rescued by Mrs. Joyce at the risk of burning her hands. Stanislaus Joyce says that this incident (in 1909 or 1910) concerned *Dubliners* and that it was Joyce's sister Eileen (Mrs. Schaurek) who rescued the manuscript. He adds that Joyce gave her a pair of gloves in gratitude. Joyce's own version of this episode was written to Harriet Shaw Weaver on January 1, 1920, at the time he gave her the final manuscript of *A Portrait:* "The 'original' original [of *A Portrait*] I tore up and threw into the stove about eight years ago in a fit of rage on account of the trouble over *Dubliners.* The charred remains of the MS were rescued by a family fire brigade and tied up in an old sheet where they remained for some months. I then sorted them out and pieced them together as best I could and the present MS is the result." Miss Weaver comments: "I suppose that this is the most authentic story of all."

4. *Exiles* (1918).

a. A blue notebook, 28 x 20 cm., on 32 pages of which are notes, fragments of dialogue, thumbnail sketches, etc., for *Exiles.* This manuscript is listed in the La Hune Catalogue of Joyce's Paris Library, No. 240, and is now in the Lockwood Memorial Library, University of Buffalo. It was used in the preparation of a new edition of *Exiles* published in 1951 by the Viking Press, New York. See A 16.

b. The final manuscript of *Exiles* is described in the sale catalogue of John Quinn's Library (1924), No. 4929:

> Written on 164 pages, together with title-pages and page of characters, 169 pages in all . . . The complete manuscript, beautifully written in the author's unusually legible hand. Each of the title-pages is inscribed: "*Exiles: a play in three acts. By James Joyce,*" and at the foot of each of these title-pages Joyce has written: "*Present address: Seefeldstrasse F* [*sic*] 3[iii], Zürich: Switzerland."

This manuscript was bought at the Quinn sale by James F. Drake, Inc., and is now in the library of a New York collector. Joyce had sent the manuscript to Quinn in May 1917 in return for financial assistance.

c. Corrections to *Exiles.* In a letter to Grant Richards, June 6, 1918, Joyce calls attention to two mistakes. This letter is in the Slocum Library. The greater part of the Grant Richards correspondence is in the Houghton Library, Harvard University. A few letters are in the Slocum Library, and others, including the earliest, are in the Berg Collection of the New York Public Library.

A letter from Joyce to his agent J. B. Pinker, June 9, 1918, calls attention to three mistakes in the English text. Subsequently he says these mistakes are not in the American edition, but actually only one was corrected. When the Pinker firm went bankrupt in the early 30's, this letter with the rest of the Pinker correspondence was bought up by London dealers. The larger portion of the Joyce correspondence, including the above letter, was sold by a London dealer to John J. Slocum, acting for the Gotham Book Mart, New York, in 1941.

5. *Ulysses* (1922).

a. Manuscript described in the catalogue of the Quinn sale (1924), No. 4936:

Original autograph manuscript of "Ulysses", written on over 1200 pages. In four blue morocco slip cases . . . The first slip case contains: Part I: Telemachus, Proteus, Nestor. Part II: Calypso, Lotus Eaters, Hades, Eolus, Lestrygonians, Scylla and Charybdis. The second slip case contains Part II, continued, made up of the following: Wandering Rocks, Sirens, Cyclops, Nausikaa, Oxen of the Sun. The third slip case continues Part II and contains: Penelop [*sic*], Ithaca, and Part II down to page 618 of the book. The fourth slip case contains from page 618 to the end of the work.

In March 1920 Joyce wrote to Quinn agreeing to sell him the manuscript of *Ulysses* for an unspecified sum. The following November he wrote as follows:

I began *Ulysses* in 1914 and shall finish it, I suppose, in 1921. This is, I think, the twentieth address at which I have written it—and the coldest. The complete notes fill a small valise, but in the course of continual changings very often it was not possible to sort them for the final time before the publication of certain instalments [in the *Little Review*]. The insertions (chiefly verbal or phrases, rarely passages) must be put in for the book publication. Before leaving Trieste I did this sorting for all episodes up to and including *Circe*. The episodes which have the heaviest burden of addenda are *Lotus-eaters, Lestrygonians, Nausikaa* and *Cyclops*.

This passage not only is important in understanding the various states of the manuscript of *Ulysses* but it also presages Joyce's almost continual additions and elaborations to the various states of *Finnegans Wake.*

Joyce was very much upset when he heard of the sale of the *Ulysses* manuscript to A. S. W. Rosenbach for $1,975. He wrote Quinn imploring his help to get Rosenbach to relinquish the manuscript and offered to pay any reasonable amount from money recently given him by Harriet Shaw Weaver. Joyce also wrote: "It must be understood, however, that I will not write in any pages on the MS. to 'complete' it. The additions were made by me on printed proofs."

In his letters to Miss Weaver beginning February 8, 1924, Joyce made it clear how much he resented the sale of *Ulysses* by Quinn.

Mr. Quinn sold the MS of *Ulysses* on 14 January. I waited for three days and then cabled. There was no reply. Several friends here cabled to New York but it was impossible to find out anything. At last after ten days a letter came from him saying he had sold the MS. for $1975 ($25 under the minimum price he had fixed) and on the same day at the same sale bought back two MS. poems of Meredith (50 pp.) for $1400. He added that the buyer Mr. Rosenbach would pay in six months and said he would then send me a check for half the profits less auctioneers' fees and not counting $9.,—price of the covers in which the manuscript was laid. I replied declining to accept any money and asking what is Mr. Rosenbach's price for delivering up the MS. Apart from annoyance in being balked in certain plans I had made I consider such a sale now and by a wealthy man (who had made me part owner of the MS. before the sale) a grossly stupid act which is an alienation of valuable property. It is a pity I was obliged to write such a letter but what is one to do when a MS. of 500,000 words is sold by an admirer who on the same day buys back a few pages of not very meritorious verse by a prose writer for almost the same sum?

A few months later Joyce wrote to Miss Weaver: "Dr. Rosenbach sent me a message asking me what would be my price for the corrected proofs of *Ulysses.* When he receives a reply from me all the rosy brooks will run dry.

"*Rosy Brook he bought a book*
Though he didn't know how to spell it.
Such is the lure of literature
To the lad who can buy it and sell it."

A few weeks later he wrote Miss Weaver on the subject again:

I see that Dr. Rosybrook bought a weather-beaten timetable a few days ago in London for $155,000. I cannot understand Mr. Quinn's act unless his mind was failing in some way. He does not seem to have understood my feelings, to judge by his reply to my letter, but I am just as glad my language was polite and guarded. It is regrettable but Dr. R's appearance in the composite photograph of Ulysses and equipage at the last moment is ludicrous—and monstrous when he walks off with the vessel's bill of lading under his arm.

Finally, the matter that really bothered Joyce came out in a letter to Miss Weaver discussing Quinn's death and re-introducing the matter of the sale: "It seemed to me a lamentable affair in every way and, so far as I am concerned, it did me a fair amount of harm with a public which values people by sales."

The Rosenbach estate still has the manuscript of *Ulysses.*

b. The following are the 11 manuscripts of *Ulysses* in Joyce's Paris Library now in the Lockwood Memorial Library, University of Buffalo. Descriptions are taken from the La Hune Catalogue, 1949, Nos. 252–9, and from hasty notes made by one of the compilers during a private examination of the library in the spring of 1949. Page numbers refer to the first Shakespeare and Company edition of *Ulysses.*

b.i. Manuscript notes for the following episodes, in order: Eumaeus, Circe, Nausicaa, Wandering Rocks, Hades, Oxen of the Sun, Cyclops, Ithaca, and Scylla and Charybdis; in a 40-page notebook lacking covers, with some pages blank.

ii. Proteus episode. A complete early version, on 18¼ pages of a notebook, 23 x 19 cm., with an orange-red cover. Many marginal corrections.

iii. Scylla and Charybdis. Fragmentary conversations, which appear altered in the final version; on 10 large unlined leaves, with a single exception written on one side only.

iv. Sirens. Page 265 to the end, in a blue notebook, 23 x 19 cm., containing 12 closely written leaves, many written on both sides.

v. Cyclops. Pages 306, 309, etc.; 2 very large leaves of foolscap folded to 8 closely written pages.

vi. Nausicaa. Pages 331–47; in a red-covered notebook, 23 x 19 cm., 20 pages, with many marginal notes.

vii. Oxen of the Sun. Approximately pp. 366–75; in a blue-covered notebook, with "No. 1" written on the cover, 24 x 20 cm. Ten numbered pages written on one side only but with the opposite pages filled with corrections.

viii. Oxen of the Sun. Approximately pp. 375–87; in a brown-covered notebook, 23 x 16 cm. The pages are numbered 11 to 23, continuing the preceding. There are 2 additional pages of inserts and many corrections on opposite pages.

ix. Oxen of the Sun. Pages 379–82; in a brown-covered notebook, with "No. VI" written on the cover, 20 x 15 cm. The pages are numbered 1 to 5, and there are pencil alterations on one opposite page.

x. Oxen of the Sun. Approximately pages 387–94; in a gray-covered notebook, with "No. VIII" written on the cover, 20 x 15 cm. Ten leaves, of which 9 contain the manuscript; 6 facing pages contain pencil and ink corrections. This is a later version of *b.viii,* above.

xi. Circe. In a tan-covered notebook, 21 x 16 cm., containing 40 leaves, of which there are 13 numbered rectos and 20 unnumbered pages containing text. This is one of the first versions of this episode, as it ends as follows: "Schema, Money Talk, Fortune Telling, . . . (?) flies, Dance of Hours, S.D.'s mother, transformation scene."

In a letter to John Quinn, January 1921, Joyce wrote: "I wrote the Circe episode nine times from first to last."

c. Cyclops. Described in Sylvia Beach's catalogue of 1935, No. 3, as follows: "Holograph manuscript of the first draft of the *Cyclops* episode, in copybook with blue covers, 8½ x 7 ins., 35 closely written pages, in ink, crossed off in red pencil. On front cover of copy-book, white label with initials 'J.J.' stamped in black." This manuscript is in Miss Beach's library.

d. Penelope. Typescript of *Penelope.* Twenty pages, 21 x 17 cm., numbered 1–12, 14, 17–18, 21, 23–6. Beginning "Yes because he never did a thing like that" (p. 690 of the Shakespeare and Company edition, 1922) and ending "or the voice either comes lo-ove's" (p. 713, l. 33). Profusely corrected throughout in ink by Joyce, with long passages written in his hand to be inserted. About the first half of the *Penelope* episode, differing from the text of the first edition.

This manuscript is described in C. A. Stonehill, New Haven, Connecticut, Catalogue, 1936, item No. 160, and is now in the library of a Missouri collector.

e. Proofs of *Ulysses* described by Sylvia Beach in her catalogue of 1935, No. 2, as follows:

A complete set, and several incomplete sets of the proofs abundantly corrected and added to by the author. About 600 pages contain 5 to 10 lines of autograph corrections, others are almost completely covered with manuscript. These proofs show the important changes that James Joyces [*sic*] made in his "Ulysses" while it was printing, and his manner of continually adding text to successive sets of proofs up to the very moment before going to press. They are treasures of inestimable value for "Ulysses" lovers.

These proofs were purchased from Miss Beach by a New York collector who deposited them in the Houghton Library, Harvard University. They were studied by Joseph Prescott in the preparation of his unpublished doctoral dissertation "James Joyce's *Ulysses* as a Work in Progress," Harvard University, 1944.

f. Proofs of *Ulysses* described in the private catalogue of the owner Edward W. Titus as follows:

Complete and final proofs of the first edition of this stupendous work with the author's profuse autograph corrections, emendations and additions exceeding sometimes 160 words on a single page. These important additions are not found in the manuscript of the work, that had been the sensation of the memorable Quinn Sale in 1924. Nor do they include mere corrections and instructions to the printer in the author's hand, with which these proofs abound also. This set of proofs made up in book form contains no less than 50 autograph signatures of James Joyce in his o.k. for press. These signatures are invariably accompanied by Miss Beach's, the publisher.

In a letter to Miss Weaver in March 1927 Joyce wrote: "Somebody has taken from the works at Dijon the complete final proofs of *Ulysses* corrected by me copiously and signed by Miss Beach and me (her property) and a dealer here is offering them for sale. Mr. Darantière has been telegraphed for." Two weeks later the *Chicago Tribune* (Paris edition), in "Latin Quarter Notes," by Alex Small, reviewed the affair:

It seems that the first proofs of that work, the ones marked with Joyce's OK and his corrections, found their way into the hands of a dealer who in turn sold them to an American bookseller of the left bank. Whereupon another bookseller of the left bank (this one not American), claimed proprietary rights, and began a correspondence in which insinuations and threats of legal action took the place of disinterested love of art. So far the American bookseller has the better of it, for he has sold those proofs for a fat price and they are now on their way to New York.

Actually Titus retained the proofs until 1951 when they were sold with his library at Parke-Bernet Galleries on October 8, 1951, item

No. 332. At that sale they were purchased by Jacob Schwartz for $2,300. Prior to his purchase of the proofs Schwartz told the compilers that he believed that some portions of the manuscript corrections were not in Joyce's hand and also stated that Titus bought the proofs from a representative of the Darantière firm, the printers of *Ulysses.*

g. Miscellaneous page proofs, typed manuscript pages, etc. Sylvia Beach in her catalogue of 1935, item No. 6, lists: "A selection of typescript pages with autograph corrections by the Author, from 5 to 15 lines per page. These pages may be acquired separately by those who might like to enrich their copy of 'Ulysses' with a little manuscript of Joyce."

The La Hune Catalogue, 1949, No. 263, lists proofs of the first 6 pages and of pages 561–4 of *Ulysses* with Joyce's manuscript corrections; presumably these belonged to Sylvia Beach.

The Slocum Library contains page proofs 161 to [176] with corrections and insertions in Miss Beach's hand and the printing O.K. and signature of Joyce. The Pierpont Morgan Library, New York, has pp. 629–30, 631–2, partly in manuscript and partly in typescript. The above typescript pages and odds and ends of proof are without doubt scattered all over Europe and America.

6. *Pomes Penyeach* (1927).

a. The La Hune Catalogue, 1949, of Joyce's Paris Library, No. 176, lists a blue notebook with the cover title "Verses," containing 11 of the 13 poems in manuscript, omitting "A Prayer" and "A Memory of the Players in a Mirror at Midnight." These poems are written on twelve and a half pages. Also included is a translation by Joyce from the German of the poem "Lament for the Yeomen," by his Zurich friend Felix Béran. This notebook is now in the Lockwood Memorial Library, University of Buffalo.

There are variations in the texts, and apparently the poems are dated by time of inspiration rather than composition, as in the published versions (i.e., there is a possibility that they are "epiphanies" in verse). If this is the case they provide important biographical references to emotionally significant events in Joyce's life.

b. Manuscript of 10 of the 13 poems of *Pomes Penyeach.* Title page and 3 poems, "Tilly," "Tutto è Sciolto," and "Nightpiece," 31 x

21 cm. "Nightpiece" is signed *J.J.* and at the bottom of the page is the following autograph note by the author to his publisher: *I hope this is right. I have mislaid the MS. Can you read it and type it* Seven poems, "She Weeps over Rahoon," "Flood," "Simples," "On the Beach at Fontana," "Alone," "A Memory of the Players in a Mirror at Midnight," and "Banhofstrasse [*sic*]." These 7 poems are on oblong sheets of gray paper, approximately 13.5 x 21.2 cm.

This manuscript is accompanied by a complete set of typescripts (a number of poems duplicated), numbered and dated by Joyce (1904–24) in blue or red pencil, with the name of the place where each poem was written. Two of the typescripts contain autograph corrections by the author. This manuscript was described by Sylvia Beach in her catalogue of 1935, No. 15, and is now in the library of a Missouri collector.

c. Joyce made a copy of these poems for the Obelisk Press edition of 1932 in order that his daughter Lucia might do illuminated initials for them. This copy was put up for sale at the Salle Drouot with the rest of Joyce's library on March 7, 1941, during the German occupation of Paris. Mme Lucie Noel in her *James Joyce and Paul L. Léon: The Story of a Friendship*, New York, 1950, p. 39, states that she and her husband Paul L. Léon went to the sale prepared to buy back as many of the books and manuscripts as possible for Joyce's family.

> He [Paul L. Léon] was able to buy back all that he considered worthwhile with the exception of one book. This was a copy of *Pomes Penyeach* with original lettrines by Lucia Joyce. A Rue de Seine bookseller went up to five thousand francs and made it clear that he was ready to go higher. Paul was very distressed. He knew who the man was and told me his name. But I have forgotten it, and I do not think that after all these years I would recognize the man—all I can remember is that he was blond and fat.

The Paris dealer who purchased this manuscript still has it in his personal library.

d. Manuscript of "Simples," one page, folio, signed, was sold at auction by G. A. Baker & Co., New York, September 10, 1940. It was bought in by the owner James Dooher and sold to the Gotham Book Mart, New York. This manuscript was later purchased by a private collector and inadvertently destroyed.

e. The Harriet Monroe Collection of Modern Poetry in the Library of the University of Chicago contains a manuscript of "Flood."

7. *Finnegans Wake* (1939).

The manuscript of *Finnegans Wake,* as the following description will bear out, does not present the same problems as the other Joyce manuscripts. The largest part of it is in the British Museum Library. Not listed here is a 120-page version of the whole book which Eugene Jolas said Joyce wrote within a few weeks during a stay on the Riviera in 1922 and gave to him. This was subsequently lost when the Jolas library was stolen at the time of the German occupation of Paris. Also not listed here is a manuscript of 150 pages which a Paris bookseller says he purchased from two book scouts who bought it at the Salle Drouot sale of Joyce's effects in 1941.

a. The bulk of the notes, earliest drafts, typescripts, corrected proofs, etc. (weighing 54 pounds), were given to the British Museum in July 1951 by Harriet Shaw Weaver who was given them by Joyce in an attempt to repay her incredible generosity to him. The list which she prepared for the compilers of this bibliography occupies 21 pages of typescript and shows that the manuscript is lacking only in Part II. Miss Weaver's list is here summarized and paraphrased for the sake of brevity; an attempt has been made to list the most interesting material, but it must be emphasized that this is only a fragment of the whole. In many cases the most interesting additions occur on the typescript and galley proofs.

i. Part I. The whole of Part I except i and vi is in a large red-backed notebook, probably the earliest manuscript notebook of *Finnegans Wake,* dating from the autumn of 1923.

ii. Part I.i. This occurs at the end of a notebook containing Part III.iv, dating from the autumn of 1926. Miss Weaver writes:

> It is remotely founded on a paragraph about a giant's grave in a small pamphlet (now undiscoverable) on St. Andrew's Church, Penrith, Cumberland (written early in this century by the then vicar of the church and sent by me to Mr. Joyce in the early autumn of 1926). The pamphlet contained a mention of a curious barrow or mound in the churchyard which local tradition maintained was the burial place of a giant of prehistoric Britain.

iii. Part I.v. This section in the above notebook is referred to by Joyce as "The Hen." Under this heading Miss Weaver refers to a "curious letter" in the notebook, written by an earlier incarnation of

Anna Livia Plurabelle to "Mr. Earwicker." Miss Weaver writes: "The writing of this epistle must have amused Mr. Joyce but he does not seem actually to have used much of it."

iv. Part I.vi. A black notebook containing the earliest draft (but not "The Mookse and the Gripes," which was not written until after the rest of the piece had appeared in *transition*) plus a pencil draft of "The Mookse and the Gripes."

v. Part II. This section is not so completely represented as Parts I and III and, with the exception of isolated passages, is not dated.

vi. Part II.i. Incomplete drafts, fair copies and typescripts.

vii. Part II.ii. The middle pages (FW 282–304) are complete in a large notebook. These were written in 1926 and called "The Triangle," later "The Muddest Thick That Was Ever Heard Dump." The rest of the episode is incomplete and was written after Part III.

viii. Part II.iii. The King Roderick O'Conor piece (FW 380–2) was the first piece of *Finnegans Wake* written. On March 11, 1923, Joyce wrote to Miss Weaver: "Yesterday I wrote two pages—the first I have written since the final *Yes* of *Ulysses*. Having found a pen, with some difficulty I copied them out in a large handwriting on a double sheet of foolscap so that I could read them." That double sheet, very much written over, containing the King Roderick O'-Conor piece, was typed out for Joyce by Miss Weaver, together with three other early sketches, when he was in England in July–August 1923.

ix. Part II.iv. This section represents the fusing of two episodes, Mamalujo, in a large notebook which dates from late 1923, and Tristran and Isolde, of which Miss Weaver writes:

> was written, I think, in July 1923 when Mr. Joyce was staying at Bognor in Sussex. At any rate I typed it for him in August 1923 from his fair copy and he then gave me that fair copy and the first drafts. I think he must have mislaid the typescript or forgotten about it, for this episode was never printed as it stood and it was not 'til July 1938 that Mr. Joyce asked for a new copy of the typescript when working on Part II.iv.

She adds that not much of "Tristran and Isolde" was used by Joyce.

x. Part III.i, ii, iii. These sections, dating from 1924, are in a large green notebook. In the same notebook are the first fair copies of i and ii.

xi. Part III.i. "The Ondt and the Gracehoper"; the earliest draft is separate in a pink notebook.

xii. Part III.iv. This section is contained in a large notebook with the mathematical lesson "The Muddest Thick That Was Ever Heard Dump" and early drafts of Part I.i.

xiii. Part IV. Miss Weaver writes:

There are not so many early drafts and fair copies in manuscript of this last and shorter part of the book. The first drafts, with insertions on their back pages, seem to have been typed immediately and then worked over by Mr. Joyce who, besides making very numerous insertions throughout, also appended manuscript pages. These were typed out again and again, with additions each time . . . Part IV seems to have been written in 1938, except for two short passages dating from the summer of 1923; one of them about S. Kevin (now expanded, FW 604–606), the other about "pidgin fella Berkeley" and S. Patrick (now FW 611–612).

b. Fifty-eight small notebooks, listed in the La Hune Catalogue of Joyce's Paris Library, 1949, No. 157, and now in the Lockwood Memorial Library, University of Buffalo. A cursory examination showed them to be fragments of *Finnegans Wake,* all apparently composed when Joyce's sight was extremely poor, for they contain fragmentary notes, paragraphs composed from these notes, and then longhand copies probably in the hand of Madame France Raphaël. These paragraphs were then apparently used in composing some of the later (to be written) passages of *Finnegans Wake.*

c. Miscellaneous manuscripts of *Finnegans Wake.* The five book and innumerable magazine appearances of it as *Work in Progress* all had to be set up in proof before publication, and as Joyce was accustomed to compose on proof, there are doubtless many significant proofs still in existence. The Slocum Library contains the copy of *transition* that was used to set up the Crosby Gaige *Anna Livia Plurabelle,* 1928. It shows many additions and is signed by Joyce. Similarly a New York bookseller has or had corrected proofs of *Tales Told of Shem and Shaun.* There must be in circulation manuscripts of those sections not in Miss Weaver's possession. For example, two pages of Part II.i, described as appearing on p. 256 of *Finnegans Wake,* were recently offered for sale by another New York bookseller. A New York collector has three variant typescripts of the opening pages of Part II.iii, which appeared in *transition,* Paris, 26 (Winter 1937) 35–52.

d. The "Unslow, malswift" passage which is quoted by Robert McAlmon in his article "Mr. Joyce Directs an Irish Word Ballet" in

Our Exagmination Round His Factification . . . , Paris, 1929, p. 109, but which never appeared in *Finnegans Wake*. Of this passage Miss Weaver wrote on September 17, 1950:

You ask why I did not mention the "Unslow, malswift" passage in my index [of *Finnegans Wake* manuscripts]. I was not aware that Mr. Joyce had ever intended to include this in his book. He sent it to me in October 1928, saying in his letter: "I will send you in a day or two the only thing I have written in the last four months, a short description of madness and blindness descending upon Swift composed in what Gilbert calls the damned trinity of colours, with a commentary. It is just forty-seven times as long as the text." It does not appear anywhere in the MSS. The "47" is something of an exaggeration, as you can imagine.

MANUSCRIPTS OF OTHER WRITINGS

8. OSCAR WILDE: IL POETA DI SALOME. *Il Piccolo della Sera*, Trieste March 24, 1909. Neither the manuscript nor the printed version of this article, both in Italian, has been seen by the compilers. A typescript of the article in Italian and an English translation, both made in 1950, are in the Slocum Library. The manuscript is in the library of a European collector.

9. LA COMETA DELL' "HOME RULE." *Il Piccolo della Sera*, Trieste, XXIX (Dec 22, 1910) 1. Manuscript on 12 leaves, approximately 21 x 17 cm., numbered in pencil. The handwriting resembles that of the Synge translation (E 11.*b.vi*), but the signature at the end, *James Joyce* , is either in another hand or carefully rounded out to avoid misspelling by the Italian printer. In the Slocum Library.

10. HERBERT GORMAN, *James Joyce: His First Forty Years*, 1924, pp. 34–6 (B 6): Joyce's letter to the press of August 1911 concerning the publishing history of *Dubliners*. This letter had previously appeared in the *Northern Whig*, Belfast, *Sinn Fein*, Dublin, the *Egoist*, London, etc. The location of the original manuscript is unknown, but a copy of the original mimeographed pages of the letter as Joyce circulated it is in the Berg Collection of the New York Public Library.

11. HERBERT GORMAN, *James Joyce*, 1939 (B 23).
The enormous amount of manuscript material quoted or described in Gorman will be divided into three categories: juvenilia, 1892–1904; occasional writings or uncollected letters, 1904–22; occasional writ-

ings after 1922. Within this framework the material will be considered chronologically. No mention is made of the manuscripts of early periodical writings; none are known to exist.

a. Juvenilia, 1892–1904.

i. Details of the Parnell Pamphlet (*Et Tu, Healy!*) are given in the section of separate publications by Joyce (A 1).

ii. There is still no trace of Joyce's schoolboy essays.

iii. The translations of Horace and Verlaine, a letter to Ibsen, and a letter to his mother have all disappeared.

iv. *Moods* and *Shine and Dark.* These two early collections of verse that Gorman said Joyce gave to his friend George Clancy when they were students at University College have both disappeared. Mrs. Clancy says that they were not in her husband's possession at the time of their marriage (sometime before 1910). Recently Stanislaus Joyce has stated that all these early poems were burned by his brother, except the "villanelle" from *A Portrait of the Artist as a Young Man* (H 22) and the translation from Verlaine. Joyce also stated that some of the poems of *Moods* were copied out by George Clancy's younger brother. Mrs. Clancy, however, says that all her husband's brothers are dead and that it would be impossible to trace their effects.

v. The five-act play *A Brilliant Career,* which Joyce sent to William Archer, was destroyed by the author, according to Stanislaus Joyce. A letter from Archer to Joyce, September 15, 1900, discussing this play in detail is in the Slocum Library. A few sentences from this letter are quoted in Gorman, 1939, p. 68.

vi. The Paris notebook, to which Gorman gives the general title of "Memorabilia" and which was apparently continued into the Trieste period, consisted of notes on odd-sized scraps of paper. The notes for February 13 and March 6, 1902 (Gorman, 1939, pp. 96–8), are on two sides of a single sheet of ruled paper, approximately 33 x 20 cm., while the note for November 7, 1904, is on a sheet of letter paper, approximately 17 x 12 cm. The location of the other entries is unknown, but it is believed that they may have been (and may still be) in the possession of a private owner. Gorman has stated in conversation with the compilers that he used all the material made available to him with the exception of a few business accounts from the Paris period. The Paris notebook is not included in the material deposited by Mme Paul L. Léon (Lucie Noel) in the National Library of Ireland. For a more detailed description of this material see Section G.

vii. The Holy Office. Manuscript on 2 leaves, approximately 33 x 20 cm. It is signed *Jas A Joyce.* No date or place is given. There is a couplet added to p. 1 and a single correction on p. 2. A letter from a Dublin printer to Joyce (see separate publications by Joyce, A 2) indicates that this poem must have been written prior to August 17, 1904. Acquired from a private owner by the Slocum Library.

viii. The translation of Gerhart Hauptmann's *Vor Sonnenaufgang* was sold as a part of the Quinn library in January 1924 and was purchased by the Brick Row Book Shop, New York. It appeared again in the auction rooms at the Miller-McVeagh sale at the American Art Association and Anderson Galleries on December 6, 1934, and was at that time purchased by a Detroit dealer for its present owner who now lives in Missouri.

This manuscript translation is described in the Quinn Catalogue, No. 4939, as follows:

Autograph manuscript of his translation of Gerhart Hauptmann's "Before Sunrise," written on pages numbered 1–198, inclusive, in a small quarto black oil-cloth-covered notebook, dated Summer, 1901. In a cloth slip case. The complete manuscript entirely in the handwriting of Joyce, without corrections, and with portions scored in red ink. It is initialed by Joyce at the end. This translation has never been published.

The catalogue of the Miller-McVeagh sale gives this further description: ". . . small quarto about 24,000 words. Signed at the end, 'J A J', and dated July 23, 1901. Inscribed: 'Summer, 1901. MS/Mullingar. Westmeath. Original by S. Fischer. Berlin 1889."

ix. The location of the manuscripts of the translation of Gerhart Hauptmann's *Michael Kramer* (two versions) is unknown. Joyce may have confused one of them with *viii*, above, when he wrote Ezra Pound, November 12, 1937:

Could you give me a word of introduction to Gerhart Hauptmann! When I was a boy in Dublin I made a translation (!) of his *Michael Kramer* a play which I still admire greatly. Perhaps he would do me the honour and pleasure of signing it—his text, I mean, not my well meant translation which some U.S. buyer obtained by stealth, I suppose, from some conniving relative of mine in the old town. He is, or was, a neighbor of yours and I think you told me you knew him.

Joyce duly received his book back inscribed by Hauptmann: "Nie hat dieses Buch einen besseren Leser gehabt, als James Joyce." See the

The Holy Office [insertion, marked *: Bringing to tavern and to brothel / The mind of witty Aristotle.]

Myself unto myself will give
This name — Katharsis-Purgative.
I who dishevelled ways forsook
To hold the poets' grammar-book
Lest bards in the attempt should err,*
Must here be my interpreter.
Wherefore receive now from my lip
Peripatetic scholarship
To enter heaven, travel hell,
Be piteous or terrible,
One positively needs the ease
Of plenary indulgences.
For every true-born mysticist
A Dante is (unprejudiced)
Who safe at ingle-nook by proxy
Hazards extremes of heterodoxy
Like him who finds a joy at table
Pondering the uncomfortable.
Ruling one's life by common sense
How can one fail to be intense?
But I must not accounted be
One of that mumming company —
With him who hies him to appease
His giddy dame's frivolities
While she consoles him when he whinges
With gold-embroidered Celtic fringes —
Or him who sober all the day
Mixes a naggin in his play —
Or him whose conduct 'seems to own'
His preference for a man of 'tone' —
Or him who plays the ragged patch
To millionaires in Hazelhatch
But weeping after holy fast
Confesses all his pagan past —
Or him who will his hat unfix
Neither to malt nor crucifix
But show to all that poor-dressed be
His more than Spanish courtesy —
Or him who loves his Master dear —
Or him who drinks his pint in fear —
Or him who once when snug abed
Saw Jesus Christ without his head
And tried so hard to win for us
The long-lost works of Aeschylus.
But all these men of whom I speak
Make me the sewer of their clique.
That they may dream their dreamy dreams
I carry off their filthy streams.

FIRST PAGE OF THE MANUSCRIPT
OF *The Holy Office.*
E.II.*a.vii.* IN THE SLOCUM LIBRARY.

La Hune Catalogue, 1949, No. 30. The confusion of this play with the previous one is based on the fact that about this time the present owner of the *Vor Sonnenaufgang* manuscript received a letter from Paul L. Léon offering to exchange an inscribed copy of *Ulysses* for the manuscript.

x. "Epiphanies." Gorman describes these as having been written in Paris between December 1902 and April 1903. The La Hune Catalogue of Joyce's Paris Library (No. 159) describes the 15 in that collection as being written before his departure from Dublin in October 1904. The Paris Library also contains 7 brief descriptions, like the "Epiphanies" all on individual leaves. The "Epiphanies" and 7 brief descriptions are now in the Lockwood Memorial Library, University of Buffalo.

xi. For the introductory chapter to *A Portrait of the Artist as a Young Man,* submitted to W. K. Magee for publication in *Dana,* see 3.*a,* above.

b. Occasional or uncollected writings or letters (1904–22).

i. The Grant Richards letters (1905–14) are all from a group now in the Houghton Library, Harvard University. Six letters, including the earliest, are in the Berg Collection of the New York Public Library, and 20 letters and post cards (1915–18) are in the Slocum Library and were apparently not available to Gorman.

ii. The entire Stanislaus Joyce correspondence is in the possession of the recipient.

iii. The letters to Arthur Symons, "Poppie" (Sister Mary Gertrude), William Field, M.P., Maunsel, and George Roberts of that firm have disappeared.

iv. The letters to Aunt Josephine (Mrs. Murray) that survive are in the National Library of Ireland. The known letters to Michael Healy (with the exception of a post card in the National Library of Ireland) are in the Slocum Library, but the majority have disappeared. The two earliest surviving letters are from 1915 and 1920.

v. The translation of W. B. Yeats' *Countess Cathleen* has disappeared.

vi. *Riders to the Sea,* by J. M. Synge, translated into Italian by James Joyce and Nicoló Vidacovich as *La Cavalcata al Mare.* Manuscript of 26 pages on copy paper, 21.2 x 17.1 cm., numbered by scenes. First and last pages missing. The text runs from the beginning of the first speech to the middle of the first sentence of the last speech.

Scene I, pp. 2–4, Scene II, pp. 1–13, and Scene III, pp. 1–10. The manuscript is probably in the hand of James Joyce; there are light pencilings in the hand of Stanislaus Joyce and heavy pencilings in the hand of James Joyce, as well as many corrections in the text.

Stanislaus Joyce has written the compilers concerning this manuscript as follows:

The translation, as the handwriting shows, was dashed off in a few evenings in order to offer it to the Italian actor manager Sainati before he left Trieste with his company. That was before the first World War. Sainati accepted it, but difficulties with Synge's heirs stood in the way of its production. Carlo Linati said that when Duse returned to the stage she was thinking of giving it and had even begun to study the part of Moria.

On July 12, 1909, Joyce wrote Elkin Mathews, publisher of *Chamber Music*, as follows:

If you hold the Dramatic rights to *Riders to the Sea* will you kindly let me know whether Mr. Alfredo Sainati, manager of the Italian Grand Guignol Company, can produce my translation of it in Italy and on what conditions. There is no idea for the moment of the translation being published. Messrs. Maunsel of Dublin gave me to understand that they had the rights of the play and were making new arrangements with regard to it. Mr. Sainati would be glad to know definitely whether he can have it produced or not and in the meantime is holding over the translation.

This manuscript, acquired from a private owner, is now in the library of a Pennsylvania collector.

vii. The location of the Elkin Mathews letters of April 4, 1910, is unknown, but 9 other communications with this firm (1906–13) are in the Slocum Library.

viii. A mimeographed copy of the letter to the press of August 18, 1911, is in the Berg Collection of the New York Public Library. This is apparently contemporary with the original and was almost certainly one of those sent out by Joyce.

ix. The location of the manuscript of *Gas from a Burner* is unknown.

x. The manuscript of the lecture on Daniel Defoe is described in Sylvia Beach's catalogue of 1935, No. 14, as follows: "Holograph unpublished manuscript, in Italian, in two parts: 39 pages, thick white paper 8½ x 6¾ ins. Part I. with the title *Daniele Defoe I*, the following marginal note on p. 1: *Lecture delivered before the Università del*

Popolo, Trieste in 1912 (?) 1913. Signed *J.J.* and the date. Part II. with the title *Daniele Defoe II.*" This manuscript is still in Miss Beach's library.

In 1950 John J. Slocum acquired a draft of pp. 33–6 of this lecture, written on lined paper, 16.4 x 20.4 cm., apparently taken from a copybook. Text on the recto of 6 leaves. This draft was presented to Miss Beach.

xi. William Blake. Notes for this lecture, believed to be similar to the Defoe lecture above, but not written out in full, are in the library of a European collector. The lectures on Defoe and Blake were delivered by Joyce at the Università Popolare Triestina during the academic session November 5, 1911, to March 31, 1912.

xii. L'Irlanda Isola dei Santi e dei Savi. Manuscript of 44 pages, 17 x 21 cm. Text in Italian; some corrections. This lecture was probably also delivered in 1911 or 1912. Acquired from a private owner by the Slocum Library.

xiii. Hamlet. The location of the notes for this lecture is unknown. It was delivered from notes and not written out in full; the notes have probably been lost.

xiv. The conversation with Georges Borach is taken from his diary which was published in part in *Omnibus; Almanach auf das Jahr 1932.* Berlin, etc., 1932, pp. 141–2. The location of the diary is unknown.

xv. The letter to the *Journal de Genève* is in a private collection in Chicago, Illinois. A similar letter is in the Slocum Library.

xvi. The location of the manuscript of the parody of "Mr. Dooley" is unknown. A typescript of "Mr. Dooley" in its entirety (it is not printed in full in Gorman or in Budgen) is in the Slocum Library.

xvii. The translations for a Zurich newspaper were done for Felix Béran of the *Neue Zürcher Zeitung.* These translations have never been identified; it is possible that Mme Béran may have the manuscripts of some of them.

xviii. The verses "A Goldschmidt swam in a Kriegsverein," "There's a donor of lavish largesse," and "There is a clean climber called Sykes" have not been located.

xix. The verses "There's a George of the Georges named David" and "There's a hairy-faced Moslem named Simon" are in the Slocum Library.

xx. The card to Claud W. Sykes, January 2, 1918, is in the Slocum Library together with 20 post cards and letters, the majority of which date from the Zurich period.

xxi. The location of the manuscript of "The C.G. Is Not Literary" is unknown.

xxii. "The Right Man in the Wrong Place" manuscript (a parody of lines from Browning's "Pippa Passes") is in the Slocum Library.

c. Occasional writings after 1922.

i. The manuscript of the parody of Molly Brannigan has not been located.

ii. Harriet Shaw Weaver has an inscribed copy of the verse advertisement for *Anna Livia Plurabelle* in a copy of the book. Other manuscript copies probably exist.

iii. The translations of James Stephens' poem "Stephen's Green" into German, Latin, Norwegian, Italian, and French, of which only the French translation is published by Gorman, were sent to Stephens on May 7, 1932. His copy of them has disappeared. Miss Harriet Shaw Weaver has a typescript copy.

iv. The translation of the poem by Gottfried Keller has not been located.

v. A typescript copy of the "Epilogue to Ibsen's 'Ghosts' " was sent to Miss Weaver on April 9, 1934.

12. *James Joyce: Sa Vie, Son Œuvre, Son Rayonnement.* Paris, La Hune, 1949. Unless otherwise indicated the items listed below are now in the Lockwood Memorial Library, University of Buffalo.

a. The location of the letter to Lady Gregory (No. 46) is not known.

b. The letter to an unknown correspondent (No. 47) has not been traced.

c. "Quaderno" (No. 67) is a school notebook, 21 x 17.5 cm., with a white label and containing 44 pages of lined paper. On the cover is the address: "via della Sanita No. 2 Trieste Italia." On the first 13 pages are quotations from Samain, Mallarmé, Rimbaud, Bloy, and Walter Pater. Apparently a continuation of the missing Paris notebook.

d. Three notebooks from the Zurich period (No. 72).

i. A blue notebook, 17.8 x 11 cm., with a blue label, containing

14 pages of French vocabulary and colloquialisms; also 5 pages of a translation of an article on a world peace organization.

ii. A blue notebook with a white label; an exercise book in modern Greek.

iii. A blue notebook with a white label; an exercise book with notes in French, English, Greek, and Homeric words.

e. The letters from Joyce to Louis Gillet (No. 135) are in the possession of Mme Gillet.

f. The letter from Joyce to Yeats, September 5, 1932 (No. 136), declining membership in the Irish Academy of Letters is in the possession of Mrs. Yeats.

g. Three letters from Joyce to Mme Ludmilla Bloch-Savitsky, the translator of *A Portrait* into French (Nos. 222, 223), are in the possession of Mme Savitsky.

h. The correspondence of Joyce with his lawyers (No. 278). The La Hune Catalogue gives no indication of what this material includes.

i. A large notebook (No. 346), 24 x 18 cm., of 1017 pages. Joyce has written here, in longhand, copies or extracts or summaries of all his published books through *Ulysses* and some additional material. These have been copied off in a large round hand by Mme France Raphaël. There is no indication of what use Joyce made or intended to make of them, but presumably they date from the same period as the 58 notebooks described above, 7.*b*.

13. *A James Joyce Yearbook,* edited by Maria Jolas, Paris, Transition Press, 1949 (B 30).

a. Photostatic reproduction of a quotation from Edgar Quinet in Joyce's hand, between pp. 128–9. This was found among Paul L. Léon's papers and is now in the Slocum Library, through the courtesy of Mme Léon (Lucie Noel).

This passage of which Joyce was extremely fond is quoted in its entirety on p. 281 of *Finnegans Wake* and is also parodied on pp. 14–15 and 236 of that work. Writing to Harriet Shaw Weaver, November 22, 1930, Joyce says:

> The page enclosed is still another version of a beautiful sentence from Edgar Quinet which I already fashioned in *transition* part one beginning "since the days of Hiber and Hairyman, etc." E.Q. says that the wild flowers on the ruins of Carthage, Numancia, etc. have survived the political rises and falls of Empires. In this case the wild flowers are lilts of children.

Note especially the rainbow treatment of the double rainbow in which the iritic colours are first normal and then reversed.

b. Ad-Writer, p. 170. This was found among Paul L. Léon's papers and is now in the Slocum Library through the courtesy of Mme Léon.

14. *I Hear You Calling Me*, by Lily McCormack, Milwaukee, Bruce Publishing Co., 1949 (B 31).

a. The letter (Joyce to John McCormack) whose opening paragraph is quoted on p. 166 is in the possession of Mrs. McCormack.

15. *James Joyce's Dublin*, by Patricia Hutchins, London, Grey Walls Press, 1950 (B 32).

a. The limerick about Lady Gregory first appeared in print in Oliver St. John Gogarty's *As I Was Going Down Sackville Street*, New York, Reynal & Hitchcock, 1937 (B 22). No copy in Joyce's hand is known to exist.

b. The letters from Joyce to his Aunt Josephine (Mrs. Murray) are in the National Library of Ireland.

16. Periodical contributions not recorded elsewhere.

a. Ulysses, as it appeared in the *Little Review* and the *Egoist*. These were presumably typescripts made from the manuscript in the Quinn sale. They undoubtedly contained many corrections. The location of the former is not known; the latter is in the possession of Harriet Shaw Weaver.

b. The letter to Carlo Linati, reproduced in *Il Convegno*, is in a private collection in London.

c. The copy of *Ecce Puer*, reproduced in *Le Phare de Neuilly*, is possibly still in the possession of the editor of that periodical.

d. The letter to Carlo Linati, reproduced in *Prospettive*, is in the Slocum Library.

e. The letters to J. B. Pinker, published in *More Books*, are in the Boston Public Library.

f. The parody of Seumas O'Sullivan's poem, printed in the *Saturday Review of Literature*, is in the Berg Collection, New York Public Library.

g. The Joyce-Svevo correspondence, printed in *Inventario*, is in the possession of Svevo's widow Mme Livia Veneziani-Schmitz.

h. The letter to Oliver St. John Gogarty, reproduced in part in the *Saturday Review of Literature*, is in the Manuscript Division of the New York Public Library.

i. The quotations from a letter to Robert McAlmon published in the *New York Times* and *Time* are from a letter in the possession of a Yale professor who also owns the rest of the correspondence.

17. Unpublished manuscript material not mentioned in books.

a. "Giacomo Clarenzio Mangan." Incomplete manuscript in Italian of a lecture probably delivered in Trieste in 1911 or 1912 on the Irish poet James Clarence Mangan. 21 x 17 cm. Includes pp. 1–4, 6–10, 12–22, 24–6 (unfinished), one unnumbered page, and one page numbered 23, probably inserted incorrectly. With extensive marginal revisions. Much of this lecture appears to have been taken from Joyce's essay on Mangan in *St. Stephen's* (May 1902) (C 2). Acquired from a private owner by the Slocum Library.

b. Occasional or extemporaneous verse. Under this heading are listed some of the numerous parodies, limericks, or jingles that Joyce presented to his friends or sent them in letters. Others were inscribed in books; many remain to be collected.

i. Two 4-line stanzas concerning the Fay brothers (of Abbey Theatre fame). No date, but prior to October 1904. In the Slocum Library.

ii. A 4-line stanza about Stephen Dedalus is contained in a letter to Ezra Pound, dated April 9, 1917. A copy of this letter is in the Manuscript Division of the New York Public Library.

iii. A parody of "Who is Sylvia," included by Miss Beach with her copy of *Ulysses* in her catalogue of 1935, No. 1. The present location of this parody is not known.

iv. A 4-line stanza on Dr. Rosenbach. Quoted in 5.*a*.

v. A 4-line stanza parody of "Little Jim," concerning an eye clinic in Paris, was sent to Miss Weaver on April 29, 1925.

vi. A 4-line parody of "For He's a Jolly Good Fellow," concerning Samuel Roth, was sent to Miss Weaver, February 1, 1927.

vii. A 9-line poem entitled "To Budgen, Naughty Tinker," partially by Joyce, was sent to Frank Budgen during the period 1926–28 and is now in the Slocum Library.

viii. A 4-line epigram about Pound and Joyce was sent to Pound in late 1927 or early 1928 and is now in the possession of Mrs. Pound.

ix. An 8-line parody of "Father O'Flynn," concerning Ford Madox Ford, was sent to Miss Weaver on February 16, 1931. Father O'Flynn appears several times in *Ulysses.*

x. A 4-line parody of "Humpty Dumpty" was sent to Frank Budgen on September 5, 1933, and is now in the Slocum Library.

xi. Argus Books, Mohegan Lake, New York, has announced for publication *The Purlieus of Venus* which will include an 88-line poem by Joyce "to a young American girl in Paris." The manuscript of this poem is presumably in the possession of the English editor of the book, Mrs. Constance McKerrow.

xii. Sonnet in Parisian slang (*en argot parisien*) addressed to Stuart Gilbert, dated July 1, 1935, is still in Gilbert's library.

c. An early version of the first paragraph of *Finnegans Wake* with a word-for-word exposition was sent by Joyce to Miss Weaver, November 15, 1926. This alone, of the many general explanations of *Ulysses* and *Finnegans Wake* sent by Joyce to Miss Weaver, Frank Budgen, and others, is listed here, for it is unique in the amount of detail it contains and, as such, represents a separate manuscript.

d. Portion of a paper on aesthetics composed in Joyce's hand. One folio sheet written on both sides and signed twice: *JAJ 13/2/03 Paris* . and *JAJ 6 March 1903 Paris* . Accompanied by a small sheet, headed by a quotation from St. Thomas Aquinas and containing 13 lines on aesthetics, all in Joyce's hand. Signed *Pola JAJ 4.xi.04* . In the Slocum Library.

F. *Musical Settings of Works by James Joyce*

JOYCE'S LYRIC POEMS interested composers from the moment they were published. Geoffrey Molyneux Palmer, a Dublin organist and composer, wrote Joyce in July 1907, less than two months after the publication of *Chamber Music*, and asked permission to set to music six of the lyrics. In all Mr. Palmer set eight of the poems, though Joyce urged him to set the whole book, writing him on July 19, 1909:

I hope you may set all of *Chamber Music* in time. This was indeed partly my idea in writing it. The book is in fact a suite of songs and if I were a musician I suppose I should have set them to music myself. The central song is XIV after which the movement is all downwards until XXXIV which is vitally the end of the book. XXXV and XXXVI are tailpieces just as I and III are preludes.

In the fall of 1909 Joyce was in Belfast and while there met W. B. Reynolds, musical critic of the *Belfast Evening Herald*, who had already set some of the lyrics. The compositions of Palmer and Reynolds were not published. Adolph Mann's setting (listed below) was the first to reach the public.

Joyce wrote Adolph Mann on June 24, 1910: "Your setting of my song is the third I have heard. I find it very happy in tone and the sliding scale on the third line makes a very nice effect." It was, however, Molyneux Palmer's setting of the same song that Joyce preferred, and he wrote Palmer in July 1919 asking permission to use it at a concert in Zurich by an Irish baritone, Augustus Milner.

Ten years later Joyce wrote Harriet Shaw Weaver:

Herbert Hughes, the musician, was here. He took down from me at the piano my two Irish come-all-yous and is going to set them and publish them as sung by. He said he would arrange to have 5 of *Pomes Penyeach* set to music [afterward expanded into *The Joyce Book* (A 29)]. Eugene Goossens asked leave to set eight more of *Chamber Music*. Nineteen of this book were set this year so the title appears to have been justified.

In addition to the published musical settings listed below a number of important settings remain in manuscript. These include three songs from *Chamber Music:* "Sleep Now," "Gentle Lady," and "All Day," by Tibor Serly, composed in 1926, and "Silently She's Combing Her Long Hair" (*Chamber Music*, XXIV), by the same composer, written in 1927. Settings in manuscript by Sergius Kagen include "She Weeps over Rahoon," "Strings in the Earth and Air," "Rain Has

Fallen," and "O Cool Is the Valley Now." The latter is scheduled for 1953 publication.

1. OUT BY DONNYCARNEY. Song. Words by James Joyce; music by Adolph Mann. Cincinnati, etc., John Church, [1910]. 8 pp. Copyright January 19, 1910.

Chamber Music, XXXI. The first publication of Joyce in America, preceding other publications by over four years.

2. O COOL IS THE VALLEY NOW. Louis Koemmenich. New York, J. Fischer & Bro., [1919]. 6 pp. Copyright May 24, 1919.

Chamber Music, XVI.

3. GOLDENHAIR. By Elliot Griffis. New York, Composers Music Corp., [1922]. 8 pp. Copyright August 24, 1922; renewed September 9, 1949.

Chamber Music, V. The poem is printed separately on p. [2].

4. FROM DEWY DREAMS. By Eugene Bonner. London, J. W. Chester, [1924]. 10 pp. Copyright September 13, 1924.

Chamber Music, XV.

5. *Extract* (first pages) MR. BLOOM AND THE CYCLOPS. Opera upon "Cyclops" episode in James Joyce's Ulysses. George Antheil. *This Quarter* ANTHEIL MUSICAL SUPPLEMENT. *This Quarter*, Milan. 26 pp. Wrappers. Published as a supplement to *This Quarter*, Milan, 2 (Autumn-Winter 1925–26).

"Mr. Bloom and the Cyclops," *Ulysses* (RH 287, ll. 1–3, the first sentence), pp. 22–4. A photographic reproduction of an extract from Antheil's uncompleted opera based on *Ulysses*.

6. GOLDENHAIR. Song. Words by James Joyce. Music by Frank Bridge. London, Chappell, 1925. 8 pp. Copyright December 21, 1925.

Chamber Music, V. The poem is printed separately on p. [ii].

7. SLEEP NOW. By Lee Pattison. New York, G. Schirmer, [1926]. 4 pp. Copyright April 23, 1926.

Chamber Music, XXXIV.

8. STRINGS IN THE EARTH. By J. Bertram Fox. New York, J. Fischer & Bro., [1926]. 8 pp. Copyright December 31, 1926.

Chamber Music, I. The poem is printed separately on p. 1.

9. I HEAR AN ARMY. Words by James Joyce. Music by Sidney Harrison. London, J. B. Cramer, [1927]. 8 pp.

Chamber Music, XXXVI.

10. LAY OF SOLITUDE. By Creighton Allen. New York, G. Schirmer, [1929]. 6 pp. Copyright October 30, 1929.
Chamber Music, XXXV.

11. CHAMBER MUSIC. Six Songs for Medium Voice. Poems by James Joyce. Music by Eugène Goossens. London, J. Curwen & Sons, 1930. 30 pp. Copyright July 22, 1930.
Contains "Now, O now," *Chamber Music*, XXXIII; "Gentle lady do not sing sad songs," *Chamber Music*, XXVIII; "Dear heart, why will you use me so?" *Chamber Music*, XXIX; "O cool is the valley now," *Chamber Music*, XVI; "All day I hear the noise of waters," *Chamber Music*, XXXV; "I hear an army," *Chamber Music*, XXXVI.

12. FIVE SONGS FOR VOICE AND PIANO FROM "CHAMBER MUSIC" BY JAMES JOYCE. By Israel Citkowitz. New York, Cos Cob Press, [1930]. 18 pp. Copyright November 11, 1930.
Contains "Strings in the earth and air," *Chamber Music*, I; "When the shy star goes forth in heaven," *Chamber Music*, IV; "O it was out by Donneycarney [*sic*]," *Chamber Music*, XXXI; "Bid Adieu," *Chamber Music*, XI; "My love is in a light attire," *Chamber Music*, VII.

13. SEVEN POEMS BY JAMES JOYCE. Set to music by E. J. Moeran. London, Oxford University Press, [1930]. 28 pp. Copyright November 27, 1930.
Contains "Strings in the earth and air," *Chamber Music*, I; "The merry green wood," *Chamber Music*, VIII; "Bright cap," *Chamber Music*, X; "The pleasant valley," *Chamber Music*, XVI; "Donnycarney," *Chamber Music*, XXXI; "Rain has fallen," *Chamber Music*, XXXII; "Now, O now," *Chamber Music*, XXXIII. The poems are printed separately on p. [v].

14. ROSEFRAIL. Song. By E. J. Moeran. Poem by James Joyce. London, Augener, [1931]. 4 pp. Copyright October 22, 1931.
Contains "A flower given to my daughter" from *Pomes Penyeach*. The poem is printed separately on p. [4].

15. THE JOYCE BOOK. London, Sylvan Press and Humphrey Milford, Oxford University Press, [1933]. 88 pp. Copyright March 1933 in Great Britain. Edited by Herbert Hughes. For full collation see A 29.
Contains musical settings for all 13 of the poems of *Pomes Penyeach*, each by a different composer: "Tilly," E. J. Moeran; "Watching

the needleboats," Arnold Bax; "A flower," Albert Roussel; "She weeps over Rahoon," Herbert Hughes; "Tutto è sciolto," John Ireland; "On the beach at Fontana," Roger Sessions; "Simples," Arthur Bliss; "Flood," Herbert Howells; "Nightpiece," George Antheil; "Alone," Edgardo Carducci; "A memory," Eugene Goossens; "Bahnhofstrasse," C. W. Orr; "A prayer," Bernard Van Dieren. Each poem is printed separately on the page immediately preceding its musical score.

16. COS COB SONG VOLUME. Ten Songs by American Composers. New York, Cos Cob Press, [1935]. 36 pp. Copyright April 15, 1935.

Contains "On the beach at Fontana," Roger Sessions, pp. 3–6; "Gentle lady," Israel Citkowitz, pp. 11–13. From *Pomes Penyeach* and *Chamber Music*, XXVIII.

17. SHE WEEPS OVER RAHOON. Words by James Joyce. Music by Harold Triggs. New York, Galaxy Music Corp., [1935]. 6 pp. Copyright July 13, 1935.

From *Pomes Penyeach.*

18. ANNA LIVIA PLURABELLE. Text by James Joyce. Music by Hazel Felman. Chicago, Argus Book Shop, [1935]. 24 pp. Copyright January 2, 1936. Issued in an edition of 350 copies, numbered and signed by the composer. Enclosed in a paper slip case and accompanied by a 12-page pamphlet essay *Music and James Joyce*, by Martin Ross.

Contains "Anna Livia Plurabelle" (FW 215, ll. 3–216, conclusion).

19. THREE MADRIGALS. By David Diamond. New York, Edwin F. Kalmus, [1938]. 8 pp. Copyright September 15, 1938.

Contains "He who hath," *Chamber Music*, XXI; "Gentle lady," *Chamber Music*, XXVIII; "Bid adieu," *Chamber Music*, XI.

20. RAIN HAS FALLEN. Samuel Barber. Set to Poems from "Chamber Music" by James Joyce. New York, G. Schirmer, [1939]. 8 pp. Copyright September 15, 1939.

Chamber Music, XXXII.

21. SLEEP NOW. Samuel Barber. Set to Poems from "Chamber Music" by James Joyce. New York, G. Schirmer, [1939]. 6 pp. Copyright September 15, 1939.

Chamber Music, XXXIV.

22. I HEAR AN ARMY. Samuel Barber. Set to Poems from "Chamber Music" by James Joyce. New York, G. Schirmer, [1939]. 10 pp. Copyright September 15, 1939.

Chamber Music, XXXVI.

23. A FLOWER GIVEN TO MY DAUGHTER. David Diamond. Text by James Joyce. New York, Arrow Music Press, [1942]. 4 pp. Copyright July 7, 1942.

From *Pomes Penyeach*.

24. RAHOON. The Words by James Joyce. Set to Music by E. J. Moeran. London, Oxford University Press, [1947]. 8 pp. Copyright July 3, 1947.

"She weeps over Rahoon" from *Pomes Penyeach*. The poem is printed separately on p. [ii].

25. BRIGID'S SONG. David Diamond. New York, Music Press, [1947]. 4 pp. Copyright November 5, 1947.

From *A Portrait of the Artist as a Young Man* (H 22).

26. A FLOWER GIVEN TO MY DAUGHTER. Albert Roussel. Poème de James Joyce. Textes Anglais et Français. Paris, Durand, [1948]. 4 pp. Copyright April 30, 1948. French translation by Rollo H. Myers.

From *Pomes Penyeach*.

27. ULYSSES. Cantata for Tenor Solo, Chorus and Orchestra. Matyas Seiber. Words by James Joyce. London, Schott, [1948]. 84 pp. Copyright September 9, 1948.

Contains "The heaventree," *Ulysses* (RH 682–3); "Meditations of evolution increasingly vaster" (RH 683); "Obverse meditations of involution" (RH 683); "Nocturne—Intermezzo" (RH 685); "Epilogue" (RH 686).

28. RAIN HAS FALLEN ALL THE DAY. By Wm. R. Smith. Philadelphia, Elkan-Vogel, [1948]. 6 pp. Copyright September 17, 1948.

Chamber Music, XXXII.

29. SIX COMMENTAIRES pour ULYSSE de JAMES JOYCE. Thomas de Hartmann. Paris, M. P. Belaieff, [1948]. 36 pp. Copyright January 2, 1949; published in Paris in 1948. The French text is taken from the translation published by A. Monnier in 1929. In the final "Commentaire," the concluding lines of *Ulysses*, the composer includes the words "Triest-Zurich-Paris, 1914–1921."

Contains "Introduction," *Ulysses* (RH 252; Monnier 289); "Complainte du testament" (RH 200–1; Monnier 230); "Valse des heures" (RH 561; Monnier 638); "Eglogue," (RH 340; Monnier 393); "Coucou" (RH 375–6; Monnier 435); "Nuit à Gibraltar," (RH 767–8; Monnier 870). The text of the passages set to music is printed separately in English with the page numbers of the revised Shakespeare and Company edition (eighth printing and after) on p. [iv].

30. BID ADIEU. Words and Air by James Joyce. Musical Setting by Edmund Pendleton. Paris, Ars Musica, [1949]. 8 pp. Copyright. This is the only setting in which Joyce had a hand in the music.

Chamber Music, XI.

31. 4 PIEŚNI. 4 songs. Karol Szymanowski. Words by James Joyce. Op. 54. [Cracow], Polskie Wydawnictwo Muzyczne, [1949]. 12 pp. Copyright August 15, 1949.

Contains "Gentle lady," *Chamber Music*, XXVIII; "Sleep now," *Chamber Music*, XXXIV; "Lean out," *Chamber Music*, V; "My dove," *Chamber Music*, XIV.

English and Polish text. Polish translations by J. Iwaszkiewicz.

32. TRE POEMI PER UNA VOCE E ORCHESTRA DA CAMERA (Variazioni sopra una serie di dodici note). Luigi Dallapiccola. Zürich, Hermann Scherchen—Ars Viva, 1949 [*c.* 1950]. 28 pp. Reproduced from the composer's manuscript.

Pp. [4–5], "A flower given to my daughter." Text in English, Italian (translation by Eugenio Montale), Spanish, French, and German.

Pp. 6–9, song, with orchestral score and piano reduction.

33. ALL DAY I HEAR. Text by James Joyce. Music by Sergius Kagen. New York, Weintraub Music Co., [1950]. 6 pp. Copyright 1950.

Chamber Music, XXXV.

34. ALL DAY I HEAR. Words by James Joyce. Music by Gardner Read. New York, etc., Boosey & Hawkes, [1950]. 8 pp. Copyright 1950.

Chamber Music, XXXV.

35. SLEEP NOW. Sergius Kagen. New York, etc., Leeds Music Corp., [1951]. 4 pp. Copyright 1951.

Chamber Music, XXXIV.

36. RAIN HAS FALLEN ALL THE DAY. Robert Ward. New York, Peer International Corp., [1951]. 4 pp. Copyright 1951.
Chamber Music, XXXII.

37. NUVOLETTA. Samuel Barber. New York, G. Schirmer, [1952]. 12 pp. Copyright 1952.
FW 157–9, extracts only.

G. *Miscellany*

RECORDINGS

The circumstances of Joyce's recordings are unknown to the compilers. Joyce, however, made one recording from *Ulysses* and two from the last few pages of the Anna Livia Plurabelle chapter of *Finnegans Wake*. Only the second of these Anna Livia Plurabelle recordings was commercially pressed, the first being discarded because of technical imperfections.

Ulysses. This record is described in Sylvia Beach's catalogue of 1935, No. 4, as follows: "Phonograph record of a reading by James Joyce from 'Ulysses' pages 136–137, recorded by His Master's Voice on one side only; with parchment label on which is printed: *Ulysses* (pp. 136–137), *Shakespeare and Company 12, rue de l'Odéon, Paris.* Signed: James Joyce, Paris, 17 november 1926 (date of recording). Only remaining copy of the 30 that were made. Paris 1926."

This extract from the Aeolus episode of *Ulysses* includes the paraphrase of the speech that John F. Taylor delivered at the University College Debating Society. Reference is also made to this speech in Yeats' *Autobiographies* and in *The Language of the Outlaw*, [1904 or 1905], a rare leaflet by Roger Casement. The *Ulysses* recording is extremely rare. The copy described in the Sylvia Beach catalogue is now in the Poetry Room of the Lamont Library, Harvard University, and is badly worn. Other copies are in the libraries of Miss Harriet Shaw Weaver and Constantine P. Curran. Brinsley MacNamara, director of the National Gallery of Ireland, Dublin, is reported to have a copy. A few broken or damaged copies have been examined in the libraries of American collectors. It has recently been reported that a reissue of this record is being prepared in Paris.

Anna Livia Plurabelle. The recording of this passage (FW 213–16) exists in a number of different pressings: (1) Orthological Institute, London, the first pressing, made for C. K. Ogden; (2) His Master's Voice; (3) Argus Book Shop, Chicago; (4) Gotham Book Mart, New York.

RADIO BROADCASTS

This portion of the bibliography is experimental in character. Few bibliographies have listed radio performances, both because of the ephemeral nature of the medium and the fact that radio networks and individual stations are usually unwilling to have the public consult material in their files concerning original scripts or recordings. This list has been made up on the basis of letters sent to five networks. Only three of the five networks consulted were able to find references to Joyce in their files and only one of them was able to consult records prior to 1941. The compilers are deeply grateful to these networks for the information provided.

It is unfortunate that better records are not kept of literary material broadcast. Apart from its wide dissemination such material is frequently of great importance. The two-hour broadcast by B.B.C. entitled "Portrait of James Joyce," first reproduced February 13, 1950, is the most significant addition to Joyce biography in the past ten years; it includes interviews with thirty-two relatives, friends, and associates.

The following is a record of performances as reported by the various networks:

1. American Broadcasting Company. No programs.

2. British Broadcasting Corporation. Home services only, 1946–50.

Date	*Service*	*Title and Speaker*
May 17, 1946	Light	*A Portrait of the Artist as a Young Man.* Reading from Joyce's autobiography. Gerard Fay, Bill Shine.
Jan. 25, 1947	Third	*Finnegans Wake.* Talk by James Stephens.
June 11, 1947	Third	*Stephen Hero.* Book review by D. M. Davin.
June 19, 1947	Third	*Finnegans Wake.* No. 1. Talk by Walter Taplin.
Aug. 22, 1947	Third	*Finnegans Wake.* No. 2. Talk by Walter Taplin.
Jan. 10, 1948	Light	*Ulysses* reviewed in "Books and Authors" by James Stephens.
May 9, 1948	Third	"The Dead." A reading by Nathalie Moya.
June 13, 1948	Third	"Araby." A reading by C. Cusack.
Dec. 15, 1948	Northern Ireland	Irish Writers. No. 5: James Joyce. By George Buchanan.
Mar. 10, 1949	Third	Writers and Music. No. 4: James Joyce. By Sean O'Faolain.

Fly leaf: *Jas A Joyce .1901.*
Princeton University Library.

Huysmans, J.-K. *Là-Bas.* Paris, Stock, 1901.
Wrapper: *Jas A Joyce*
Fly leaf: *Jas A Joyce 1901.*
In the collection of Dr. H. K. Croessmann, Du Quoin, Illinois.

Ibsen, Henrik. *Nar Vi Döde Vågner.* København, 1899.
Signed *Jas. Joyce 1901.*
Lockwood Memorial Library, University of Buffalo.
See the La Hune Catalogue of Joyce's Paris Library, No. 34.

Moore, George. *Vain Fortune,* a novel by George Moore, with five illustrations by Maurice Greiffenhagen. New edition completely revised. London, Walter Scott, 1895.
Fly title: *Jas A Joyce March. 1901*
In the Slocum Library.

Ibsen, Henrik. *Bygmester Solness,* skuespil i tre akter. København, Gyldendalske Boghandels Forlag, 1892.
Signed *Jas. Joyce, April 1901.*
Lockwood Memorial Library, University of Buffalo.
See the La Hune Catalogue of Joyce's Paris Library, No. 32.

Tolstoy, Lyof. *The Fruits of Enlightenment,* a comedy in four acts. Translated from the Russian by E. J. Dillon; with an introduction by Arthur W. Pinero. London, William Heinemann, 1891. Wrappers.
Wrapper: *Jas A Joyce* Fly title: *Jas A Joyce April 1901*
In the Slocum Library.

Olcott, Henry S. *A Buddhist Catechism According to the Sinhalese Canon.* [London], Theosophical Publication Society, [1886?] (30th thousand).
Signed: *Jas A Joyce May.7.1901*
In the Slocum Library.

Adams, W[alter] Marsham. *The House of the Hidden Places. A Clue to the Creed of Early Egypt from Egyptian Sources.* London, John Murray, 1895.
Fly title: *Jas A Joyce 1902*
In the Slocum Library.

Fogazzaro, Antonio. *Piccolo mondo antico.* Milano, Baldini, Castoldi & C.°, 1900.
Monogram on wrapper: *JAJ*

Fly title: *Jas A Joyce 1902*

In the collection of Dr. H. K. Croessmann.

Fogazzaro, Antonio. *Piccolo mondo moderno*. Milano, Hoepli, 1901.

Fly leaf: *Jas A Joyce. 1902*

In the collection of Dr. H. K. Croessmann.

[Yeats, William Butler] *John Sherman; and, Dhoya*. London, T. F. Unwin, 1891.

Signed *Jas A Joyce* [1902] on front wrapper and title page. Parke-Bernet Galleries, New York. Catalogue of the Collection of E. W. Titus, October 8–9, 1951, item No. 713. Sold to a private owner.

PRODUCTIONS OF *EXILES*

Joyce labored heroically to have *Exiles* produced. A record of his efforts and subsequent productions is given here.

1919. Munich. Münchener Theater. Reviewed by Kurt Moreck in the *Allgemeine Zeitung*, September 7, 1919. In German.

1925, February 19—March 22. New York. Neighborhood Playhouse. 41 performances.

1926, February 14–15. London. Regent Theatre. The Incorporated Stage Society.

1926, April 3–10. Boston. The Barn. Boston Stage Society.

1930, March 9. Berlin. Deutsches Volkstheater. In German.

1930. Milan. Convegno Theatre. Reviewed in the *Corriere della Sera*, April 30, 1930. In Italian.

1945, September 11–30. London. Torch Theatre.

1947, January 6–8. New York. Hudson Park Branch, New York Public Library. Equity Library Theatre.

1948, January 18. Dublin. Gaiety Theatre.

1950, May 16. London. Q Theatre.

JOYCE MATERIAL IN THE NATIONAL LIBRARY OF IRELAND

This description of the material has been supplied by Richard J. Hayes, director of the National Library:

19 envelopes sealed containing private and business correspondence exchanged between James Joyce and Paul L. Léon in the years 1930–1940 and the latter's correspondence, business and otherwise, relating to Mr.

Joyce, his family and work. This is the property of Paul L. Léon, 27 rue Casimir, Paris. To be returned to him at his request. In case of death to be handed to Mr. James Joyce. In case of both being dead to be deposited with the National Library of Ireland, to be made accessible for literary use fifty years after Mr. Joyce's death.

This material will therefore not be available until 1991.

INDEX

This index includes all title entries, personal and proper names, periodicals and publishers. Unless page numbers are indicated, entries refer to sections (A, B, C, *etc.*) *listed in the Contents and to the number of the individual item within the section. Works by Joyce, or with contributions from him, are in small capitals; other book and periodical entries are in italics.*